Saving Our Sons

One Story at a Time

Saving Our Sons

One Story at a Time

Misty VanderWeele Presents:
Parents' stories to uplift and educate the world about
the most common muscular dystrophy, DUCHENNE

With Stories By:

Mary-Lou Weisman
Penny Wolfson
Patricia Furlong
Debra Miller

Saving Our Sons One Story at a Time

ISBN 978-0-615-47088-7

COVER PHOTOGRAPH: Andy Keller, 28, one of the older men living with Duchenne Muscular Dystrophy. Walking beside his "Uncky" is Dominik, Andy's nephew. While she was pregnant carrying Dominik, Andy's sister, Bobbi, was steadfast in her refusal to be tested as a possible carrier. As she explained, "There are no guarantees, Andy. I pray that your nephew isn't born with Duchenne. But if he is, I'll love him just as much as I love you." At six months, Dominik tested negative for Duchenne. He was a healthy little boy. "Uncky" cried when he heard the news.

To all Duchenne sons here and past

.

We, the parents, promise to FIGHT!

"One hundred years from now it will not matter how much
money was in my bank account, the sort of house I lived
in, or the kind of car I drove, but the world may be different,
because I was important in the life of a child"
~unknown

Acknowledgments

Saving Our Sons One Story At A Time has actually come together very quickly, especially considering the fact it took time to gather each story, as many hadn't come to life on paper before. Each story was crafted with tremendous amounts love and from the deep wounds of watching a child wither and weaken right before your eyes. Day by day, week to week, months into years. Not to say the journey has been all bad. I mean, after all, life has to be lived, hopefully enjoyed, as much as possible.

This brings me to the first HUGE thank you. And that is to all our Duchenne children and young adults whose life struggle remains etched into our hearts. For it is their story that forms this very book.

To my son, Luke, who changed my world forever. To my daughter and husband for all your support and patience in my mission of bringing Duchenne to the world.

From the bottom of my heart, thank you to each and every parent, grandparent and sibling who submitted a personal story from the pages of your very own Duchenne journey. I know the courage it takes to see through the pain long enough to share the good, the bad and the ugly of Duchenne. KUDDOS to YOU! This book wouldn't be a reality without your contribution and your commitment to your children.

Thank you to Debra Miller at CureDuchenne and Pat Furlong of Parent Project Muscular Dystrophy for believing in me, this book project and the meeting of the minds, if you will. You both continue to lead the Duchenne Movement. Much appreciation to be working with you!

Mary-Lou Weisman for your continued honoring of your very own son, Peter, three decades after his passing. Thank you for sharing the honest side of Duchenne life.

Dr. Charolette Thompson for your specialization and expertise in muscle disease, which lends insight into the background of Duchenne and why something must be done. You are right, we can do better!

Penny Wolfson for taking the time to share yourself and your excerpt from "Moonrise" so willingly.

To all the other parents I asked to use your writings, which helped fill in the blanks by completing the story of progression and the emotional impact Duchenne bestows upon us.

A BIG thank you to Patricia Boeckman. Your generosity and belief in me and my mission is astounding. Your friendship is cherished.

To all my Facebook friends and family for your faith in me and standing by me when it most likely would be easier to stick your head in the sand.

And last, thank you Universe for your VAST giving energy and wisdom. Ask and you shall receive.

Foreword

I am before you now, presenting this book, along with 38 other Duchenne parents. We are standing at the mountain top, staking our flag of hope and sheer down-on-our-knees urgency to save our sons. We are banding together to inspire and educate the world about Duchenne, the most common, progressive, life-expectancy-taking muscular dystrophy, in what I call the Duchenne Movement. Unless you are touched by Duchenne in some way, you most likely have no idea what Duchenne is. Actually the word "touched" is too gentle. Being touched implies a tap on the shoulder or soft caress. But I assure you nothing is further from the truth. Watching a child progress though the phases of Duchenne is more like a knife being gouged deep into the heart over and over. You don't know about the 50 years of research that still haven't rendered a cure or safe, life-saving, effective treatments. You don't know that 20,000 boys a year are being diagnosed or that, even though some boys are living into their late 20's and 30's, many are still dying on or before age 17. Duchenne reeks havoc and muscle-wasting devastation throughout childhood. Most Duchenne kids are born seemingly perfectly "normal." The parents are totally unaware their child has a terminal illness; however, by toddlerhood, muscle weakness starts its ugly appearance. The downward spiral begins: wheelchair bound by age 12, on a wing and a prayer, living to see high school graduation. Hopefully by some lucky miracle into adulthood, although almost completely paralyzed. Duchenne is an x linked, or what is referred to as a maternal linked, genetic disease, which means a woman with a Duchenne mutation is called a carrier and has a 50-50 chance of passing the disease onto a son and, rarely, onto a daughter.

The stories in this book echo the primal plea of Duchenne Parents from around the world that we need a cure, and if a cure isn't to be at this time, we want safe and viable treatments that don't cause more harm than good. This means we need pediatricians and other specialists trained in muscle disease, who know the signs, who can offer sound advice and be willing to listen and not just throw our boys into the "nothing can be done category," or worse, stereotyping the progression of Duchenne. Every boy is different. But the sooner a diagnosis can be made, the better, as Dr. Charlotte Thompson, author of *Raising a Child with Neuromuscular Disorder* blogged about: Early Diagnosis of Duchenne Muscular Dystrophy

It seems little has changed in the last fifty years for an early diagnosis to be made when a boy has Duchenne Muscular Dystrophy. This was highlighted in a recent Journal of Pediatrics article. Having cared for boys with Duchenne dystrophy in six neuromuscular programs since 1957 when I directed the muscle disease program at the University of Rochester, this is of great concern to me. Many of the boys who were referred to me had already started kindergarten. Often a teacher was the one who was concerned. This means that other boys may have been born to the parents without the help of genetic counseling. I have seen families who had three and four boys with this disorder.

The diagnosis is one of the simplest ones in pediatrics, as far as I am concerned. Fifty percent of the boys are late walkers, ie after 18 months, developmental delay is apparent in about two-thirds of the boys, they have a very specific pattern of muscle weakness, plus a markedly elevated CPK. (A blood test). The youngest boy I diagnosed without a family history was 18 months old. A very smart child development doctor referred him to me. I followed this youth for almost 28 years. He died last year.

Unfortunately, I find that pediatricians, pediatric neurologists, child development specialists and orthopedists receive almost no training in pediatric neuromuscular disorders. This causes the parents of a child with these disorders months and often years of not knowing what is wrong and keeps the child from having appropriate therapy. There is a great deal that can be done to keep boys with Duchenne dystrophy walking well into their teens and no boy with Duchenne dystrophy should be using a wheelchair by age ten. I still get e-mails from parents saying their ten-year-old boy is already in a wheelchair. We can do better than this.

Dr. Charolete Thompson
www.FindingGoodMedicalCare.com

As you read *Saving Our Sons,* you get a glimpse into the personal lives of Duchenne families. You will be taken on an emotional roller coaster ride. You will see first hand love, laughter, sheer grief and incredible amounts of courage. You will ultimately learn that, as soon as a Duchenne boy is born, he starts running out of time and many Duchenne parents start looking for a miracle.

This book is broken up into four sections following the progressive phases of Duchenne. From the beginning diagnosis, transition to a wheelchair, medical procedures, life beyond 18 and the reality of facing death much too early. I invite you to pass the book along as soon as you are done. The world MUST be educated. Lives are at risk... Time is running out!

Contents

SECTION I
The Beginning Phase: If Time Could Stand Still

Although Duchenne is genetic and present at the time of conception, one must look closely to spot muscle weakness in a baby or small child. Often times, Duchenne goes undiagnosed until around the ages of four to six. Since babies learning to walk fall down and toddlers run into things, you might not notice the walking from side to side or waddling gait. Or the unique way they get up from the floor or seated position, called gowers maneuver. Duchenne children often have enlarged calf muscles and stand with their feet a slightly apart for better balance, with their abdomen protruded out. They tire easily, which is strange for a child, and often gets mistaken for laziness. It isn't uncommon for a teacher or childcare provider to be the first to notice the difference in the Duchenne child verse others the same age. Which is the main reason prenatal or upon birth, Duchenne should be screened for, even if there isn't family history of the disease.

After the earth has opened up and swallowed you whole from the worst news a parent could hear. There is no cure, your child will be lucky to graduate high school; life does go on and from the outside looking in everything appears "normal", signs of Duchenne are slight. This phase has been referred to as the "honeymoon phase" since the child is still walking and breathing isn't compromised far from the incomprehensible death looming in the distance, knocking at the door. The Duchenne parent thinks, *if time could stand still*, the future is terrifying!

Cooper, 4 Years Old

When God gives us our children, we are not told their fate. We are not told that they will get in a car accident when they are on their way home from college. We are not told that they will get cancer at the age of 20. Unfortunately, parents of children with DMD are told that their seemingly healthy children will eventually lose all mobility. They will lose the ability to play, run with their friends, write, feed themselves, or even give you a hug. Furthermore, these parents are told that there is nothing to do to stop the progression…there is no cure. There is something terribly wrong with knowing that this is your child's future. There is something terribly wrong when you wish your child had cancer. At least if he had cancer, we would be given a treatment plan to try to "fix it."

As a parent of a child with DMD, we are left helpless. It's so easy for us to lose hope. My fear is that we will end up like so many parents who really believe they will find a cure, and 10 years from now we will end up heart broken and devastated that no cure was found. I pray that God is with these children and families and friends. We all need Him to help guide us through this life we have been given. I find peace in ,"The will of God will never take you where the grace of God will not protect you."

I know that God has never let me down before. I pray that he doesn't let me down now. I will do everything in my power to give my son the life he deserves.

On July 21, 2006, God handed us a perfect, beautiful baby boy. While Cooper developed "normally," he seemed to be hitting his physical mile-stones a little later than most children his age. He started rolling over at 8 months, crawling at 10 months, and walking alone at 17 months. The way he was developing could be considered "normal," and we and our pediatrician continued to think that he was just slightly delayed in his gross motor skills. He spoke his first words earlier than expected, knew all of his letters before his 2nd birthday and was potty trained at 2 years and 5 months. He seemed to be more advanced cognitively, so the delay in his gross motor skills was acceptable at this point.

In August, 2009, Cooper started school at The Children's House Montessori School at First Presbyterian Church in Ocean Springs, MS. He was a young 3-year-old, and had no other siblings, so there was definitely a difference in his social skills when compared to some of the other children. Cooper is a shy, sweet child who is very compliant and does not just throw himself into activities the way some of the other 3-year-olds do.

In October, 2009, Cooper's teachers went to a weekend conference. One of the speakers was Pat Furlong. She began describing early signs of children with DMD. Mary Ann, the director and head teacher at Cooper's school, immediately thought of Cooper. His symptoms at the time included: enlarged calf muscles (which are identical to his Daddy's and, in my eyes, make his legs beautiful), difficulty climbing steps and alternating feet while doing so, a bit slower on the playground, and he stood up slowly after sitting pn the floor. Mary Ann spoke with Ms. Furlong after her speech and knew she had to bring these things to our attention.

The Tuesday after the conference, I brought Cooper to school and Mary Ann asked me to come back around 2:30 for a conference. She was apprehensive about what she should say to me at this point. I spent the day worried because I knew it wasn't concerning his behavior or cognitive abilities. When I came in that afternoon, she began telling me about the conference and the speaker. She encouraged me to have a blood test to rule out a certain disease. I left the school and continued with my day as usual. I had never even heard of Duchenne's Muscular Dystrophy. I didn't know what it was and had no clue that my child could have such a devastating disease.

I got home that night, my husband and I put the kids in bed, and we talked about everything that Mary Ann and I spoke about. I got online. I searched Duchenne's Muscular Dystrophy. I completely fell apart. I didn't sleep at all that night. I cried. I lay in bed with Cooper and prayed. I cried. I lay on the couch and tried to watch television. I cried so loudly that I woke up my husband. All he could do was hold me and let me cry, and he cried with me. At 4:45 am, I called our pediatrician. She tried to comfort me. That day, she ordered his first of many blood tests.

The results of his CK test were abnormal and we were sent to a pediatric neurologist who ordered his DNA testing. On December 15, 2009, we got the results. He was positive for Duchenne's Muscular Dystrophy, with deleted exons 58-62. Where do we go from here? Of course, we started out in a depression. But we had to get ourselves together so that we could get Cooper the care that he needs. Because of some family connections, we ended up at Children's National Hospital in DC. This is where we continue to go for check-ups twice a year.

Cooper turned 4 in 2010. Once he turned 4, his doctor started him on Prednisilone. He has also started swim therapy. He is doing great. He is running now, jumping with 2 feet, climbing the steps at school, playing more on the playground, and stands much easier from a sitting position. His behavior hasn't changed, which was my biggest concern when starting the steroids. At this point, he hasn't started rapidly gaining weight. He really is doing great!

We know that this phase of his life will end before we're ready. This disease is so unpredictable. He could be mobile and active for the next 10 years, or it could end as soon as 2 years from now. We don't know. All we can do is give him the best life possible. He's such a happy child. He loves the big things in life: ferriswheels, going fast in the boat, riding his bike, swimming, playing on the playground.

It's mind-boggling to me that a child can be given the world and it will all be taken away from him because of this disease.

We watch Cooper play with his little brother, Adam, and just can't imagine that his future will be what the doctors say. It's heartbreaking for all of us, because he is such an innocent child. He and all of these sweet children are so undeserving of what their destiny is. Cooper tells us, "When I grow up, I want to be a baby doctor like Dr. Wuchi," (his pediatrician, Dr. Nnawuchi). And sometimes he asks, "Can I be a fire fighter when I grow up?" "Can I play football?" "Can I play soccer?" We all tell him, "You can be whatever you want to be when you grow up." Of course, at this point, we don't tell him what kind of disease he has.

My husband and I are so lucky to have the support of a wonderful family and many friends. His teacher, Mary Ann, is very close to our family now, along with his pediatrician. Cooper is lucky to have so many people who love him. We all want to see him grow into the amazing young man that he deserves to be.

Our family, and my business, Dreamworks Gymnastics Academy, are hosting a golf tournament on May 14, 2011. All of the money raised will go straight to research for DMD. We all must do everything in our power to help the doctors and researchers with their mission to find a cure.

Heather Clower

Nicholas, 4 Years Old

Sal and I were married in August of 2000, we both wanted children and after many failed attempts at IVF treatments, we decided to adopt. Our classes at the agency consisted of reading and listening to adopted, adoptee, and foster families speak of their experiences. We learned that our wait would most likely be at least a year or more. Little did we know a young girl had already chosen us by viewing our scrapbook. We met with her and her whole family; it was an instant bond. It was all happening so fast. About a month latter he was born at 5am in Monterey. We waited until the family was comfortable enough for us to visit. As soon as we walked into the room, his birth grandmother placed him in my arms. I immediately started to cry uncontrollably. This wasn't any child. This is my son. We were told that Nicholas wouldn't be released until Christmas Day, and this was the best Christmas gift anyone could ever get, a healthy baby boy to love and care for.

It was cold that Christmas morning and we had not slept for days. We received a call from our social worker when we were opening gifts that Nicholas would be leaving the hospital and going home to her house, in a red stocking. Nicholas' birth mother, who was very young, could not make the decision to sign relinquishment papers. So Nicholas would spend the first 3 weeks of his life in a bridge home. This decision broke my heart into a thousand pieces. I wanted his first Christmas to be in our home, his forever home.

As soon as we were done opening gifts, we ran out the door of my grandmother's home straight to our social worker's home in Carmel Valley. I held him for hours, and cried as soon as we got in the car, wanting so badly to put him in our car that had an empty car seat. Those first 3 weeks were

HELL to say the least, but I could not imagine what his birth mother was going through, I had never given birth.

After weeks of visits and daily conversations with the birth mom, social worker and foster mom, we finally got to take our beautiful son home. Our love for Nicholas was instant. From the time we first held him, he was our son, and in our hearts we were going to love him even if she decided to keep him with her.

Once he was home, we were relieved. He was here to stay. We painted his room blue and decorated it with Nemo decals. We did our best to keep all sick people away and had hand sanitizer at our front door and in his room. I was determined to have my "perfect family." No sick kids in this house!

As it happened, Nicholas got his first cold in the spring of 2007, which was not just a simple cold, it was RSV. It took months for him to recover and he was a very fussy baby. He would not sleep unless I was holding him wrapped tightly in his blanket like a burrito. This was the longest winter and spring of our life.

Finally, summer came and went, and he would then get sick again in the fall. We were told, "it's normal" for him to get respiratory infections each time he got a simple cold. It was due to the RSV. This was just going to be "how it was." This was our new normal. This was nothing we couldn't handle. So I told my husband, why not bring one more child into our crazy family.

When Nicholas was two, we talked with the social worker briefly to let her know we were considering adopting again. About 6 months later we got a call. A baby girl was born and she would be ready to go home as soon as possible. This experience was much different. We got to take our baby home straight from the hospital and surprised our whole family on Palm Sunday. She was one week old on Easter and truly was a blessing from God. She is our healthy, wild child.

That fall in 2009, all of us got a really bad cold that wouldn't go away, and Nicholas was hospitalized with pneumonia. Nicholas was turning yellow and was having his blood drawn every few days. We were so scared, I never left the hospital even when people came to try to give me a break. I would not leave my baby. After being in the hospital for one week, we met with a gastroenterologist who told us she needed to make sure he wasn't having liver failure or any other type of liver issues. She told us that his live enzymes were very high, but he was also hemolyzing and she didn't know why. We were so scared and would do whatever we needed to save my baby.

Nicholas was breathing better and was finally sent home, but not without constant visits and calls from doctors, who didn't know what was going on with him. Finally, we were sent to a hematologist, who after weeks of genetic tests for different disorders and blood work from the birth mom, diagnosed Nicholas with Beta Thalassemia Intermedia. This is a blood disorder that basically makes it look like you are anemic. You can get iron overload, which can cause a lot of health problems. The hematologist advised us that although this answered his "Anemic" issue, it didn't answer the liver enzymes.

A few months later, Nicholas was hospitalized again, this time was for a liver biopsy. It was so many months later because I was not so sure that this was safe. The procedure went well, and a few day later Nicholas' hematologist called and told us Nicholas tested positive through genetic testing for Gilbert's syndrome, and I had a meltdown in the drive through at Star Bucks. I hated myself for putting my son through all the needles and IV's and visits. I prayed while I was in that line, "God, please let me take his place. Lord, please let me suffer the physical pain." I looked back in the car seat at my son and daughter and they both smiled at me. I knew at that very moment that God had a plan. He placed both of these children in our home because he knew we would do whatever we had to do for them to live healthy and happy. We would fight for them more than anyone else would.

A few days later I got a call from our social worker. My daughter's birth mother retained an attorney and wanted her back. Well, it wasn't her who wanted her; it was the grandmother. I thought to myself, "Is this my mid-life crisis? How much more can I take? I will not give my baby up!" They were going to have to give me one hell of a fight. This was my baby! After many letters, a visit to the attorney's office and talks with social workers, not to mention so many prayers that no one could ever keep track of them, it was dropped. This was a relief that I had never felt before. I exhaled for the first time in months.

We received a call from the gastroenterologist, and she was happy to report that Nicholas' liver biopsy was completely normal and she just wanted some follow up labs at our next hematology visit. It was almost a month and I almost forgot the lab slip at home. His visit went well that day. We met with the genetic scientist, a fellow, the main doctor and his assistant. Nicholas' birth parents met us there, a little late, but they made it. They went through the whole description of the Thalassemia and what it will or could do over time as he got older. They explained that it was genetic and the chances of their next child having this was very high. Genetic counseling was in their future if they ever wanted more children. We offered to pay for whatever labs or counseling they needed.

On June 2nd I got off work a little early. I was going to make a nice dinner and stop at the grocery store before picking my babies up early from daycare. I was in the Mexican food isle, was planning on making enchiladas and my phone rang. It said , "Withheld," which meant it was one of my son's many doctors, so I answered it quickly. I heard a very shaky voice on the other end. It was my son's gastroenterologist. She said that the labs came back and Nicholas tested positive for some type of muscular dystrophy. I gasped and am pretty sure I stopped breathing. I fell to my knees in the middle of the grocery store! She told me she had already made the referral to a neurologist at the nearby children's hospital and we would see him next week.

Our visit consisted of an assessment by the fellow and then the neurologist walked in, looked at him for maybe two seconds and said, "That's Duchenne." I looked at him, very ignorant. I had never heard that word, EVER, let alone knew someone with muscular dystrophy. He told me that Nicholas will need some genetic test to confirm the diagnosis, and then we will discuss the prognosis. He called three weeks later. The test "normally" takes six weeks, but they said it was a "quick positive." Most of our family went to the next appointment and seemed very quick. Nicholas' final diagnosis is Duchenne Muscular Dystrophy, the leading genetic KILLER of boys! Nicholas has three genetic diseases which are terrible together.

It has been about one year since Nicholas' diagnosis and I now see the affects it has on my 4-year-old boy. Nicholas tiptoe walks. He gets up by either using something to pull up onto or using Gowers' maneuver and constantly complains of pain with tears that can not be stopped. Nicholas also gets very tired easily. Part of that is from the Thalassemia. Nicholas cannot ride a bike or climb up simple play structures. We our determined to make my son's life full of enjoyment, laughter, and fun, as we have in the back of our minds everyday that his life will be cut short. I cry everyday when I lie down to go to sleep and many nights I don't even go to sleep. I pray hard and often that God will help the researchers find a TRUE Cure that will END Duchenne forever so that no one else has to EVER go through this. No child deserves this pain.

Leeandra Arch Deacon

Grant, 4 Years Old

As I am writing this, he is only 4 years old. Completely happy, carefree, entirely unaware he even has a disease, and totally oblivious to the dreadful and complicated hurdles he will have to endure just to stay alive. I wish I could keep him this way, in an ignorant bliss, because the truth of Duchenne is far too much for an adult to handle, much less an innocent little boy.

I, on the other hand, am well too aware of how this disease progresses. I have read, listened, and seen far too much of the devastation Duchenne will ultimately have on a young little body. The invention of social media has been a both a blessing and a curse at the same time. On the one hand, you are able to connect with others who share the same fate; on the other, you are exposed to way too much of the ugly side of this disease way too soon-- before you are ready to come to grips with the reality that your baby's tiny body is deteriorating right before your very eyes and there is NOTHING you can do to stop it. In the early stages, it is easy to be in a sort of denial. Many of our family and friends seem to have the idea that he will miraculously recover and somehow be okay. "He looks so healthy, so vibrant, so full of life," people will tell us. Most individuals have never heard of Duchenne and don't understand its true effects. They don't take the time to read about it in a book or look it up on the internet. That is one of the most frustrating parts of this disease...no one understands it. I, of course, know the truth...NO ONE has ever survived Duchenne; NO ONE has ever recovered, gone into remission, or been okay. One hundred percent of the boys with this disease have died well before their time. Of course, I have hope for better treatments, and with some amazing research going on right now there is future hope for a cure. I lay all my hopes on a treatment and cure, and think about it when I first awake and before I close my eyes at night. Even in this day and age with so many great medical advances, I know the reality is, despite the best efforts of all the parents, the doctors, and the scientists, I have to prepare myself for the fact that the amazing treatments I read about in the scientific journals may not come in time to save Grant.

Some days I still spend wondering how this all could have happened to Grant, to my family. It is still very unbelievable to me. I did everything right, or so I thought. I went to college, got a graduate degree, got married, planned for a family, and even ate healthfully when I was pregnant. I am told by specialists, nothing could have prevented his disease. I am not a carrier for Duchenne, so no amount of testing would have found anything wrong beforehand. Grant has a completely spontaneous mutation. Our entire family was shocked at his diagnosis and we are still trying to come to terms with it. Right after learning Grant has Duchenne, I wanted to just curl up in a ball and lie in the corner, completely isolating myself from everyone and every-thing. Life wouldn't let me. I have an older son, Dresden, to take care of as well. He doesn't have Duchenne, and is a very bright, vivacious, and thoughtful boy with a promising future. There are still lunches to make, baths to give, dinners to prepare. The disease is so devious. You find out your child has a fatal disease, but when you look at him, he seems so perfect, so healthy. You are unable to wrap your mind around that contradiction. You know you have limited time and your race against this time has begun. How best to spend it? Should you fight every moment for a cure, researching, raising funds etc. or live it to the fullest, trying not to focus on the disease. Somewhere in between is the balance I am still trying to find. The phrase, "plan for the worst and hope for the best" has never had more meaning.

Since Grant's diagnosis, many things in life seem silly, mundane, and unimportant. "Who cares who wins the baseball game?" I think many times as I watch my older son at his sporting events. They are just lucky they can run. Who cares what kind of car you drive, the clothes you wear, how much money you make? None of these things matters in the least to me anymore.

Even my graduate degree and my job, which I had worked so hard at before, also became unimportant and seemed to only drain the valuable, irreplaceable time from my family. The only thing that matters now is helping Grant live his years to the fullest and putting any extra energy into doing all we can to save his life.

Many people tell me they can't even imagine being in my shoes. Honestly, I can't imagine it either. My shoes are brand new and I am still not used to wearing them. I don't want to get used to wearing them. When people ask to know the worst part, truthfully I know the worst is yet to come….he will stop walking, he will no longer be able to use his arms, he will need help to breathe and to roll over, and then his heart will fail. I usually try to spare giving out so much information to new people. I often feel like they think I am exaggerating, but that is the reality of Duchenne and it is awful. You try so hard not to think about the future, yet that is the only thing you constantly think about. Right now simple things like playing chase outside, walking to the bus stop, riding a bicycle, and climbing into the car are daunting tasks that Grant tries relentlessly to do on his own. He is such a fighter, even though his little body is silently being destroyed every time uses it. Many days I secretly wish he had ANY other disease where his hard work might pay off. With Duchenne, the opposite is true, the harder you work, the more muscle you lose. He wears himself out trying to do the things he sees his older brother doing. I find myself thinking, "How many muscle cells did he lose today from playing on the jungle gym at school, wrestling with his brother, or just walking from our car into the store?" It breaks my heart every day to watch him struggle. This is the part I cannot bear. He will not get better at riding his scooter, his tricycle, or the skateboard. He will never be able to run faster. No matter how hard he tries or how much he practices, his abilities will only decline. This is when I think, my husband is lucky, he GETS to go to work every day, so he doesn't have to witness Grant in his daily heart-wrenching struggles. Did I make the right decision to stay at home? Can my heart bear to witness his deterioration every day? It is definitely too much for anyone to bear. A paradox I find myself in daily. I want to spend every second with him, but my heart breaks to watch Duchenne steal his life away.

Thoughts of the disease cause so much negative anxiety and useless amounts of energy to build up that my husband and I found no other outlet than to start a foundation focused on raising awareness and funds to benefit Duchenne research. The Save Our Boy Foundation was created to dedicate all donations directly to research for this horrible disease. I know we can't do everything, but fill any spare time we have with events designed to bring more awareness and research funding. Many other families we have met have felt compelled to do the same after finding out that many of the larger organizations donate only a small percent of their money to Duchenne. There is a huge amount of frustration in the Duchenne community. After so many years of telethons and hundreds of millions of dollars raised, there are still no good treatments for this disease. All said, I just want a good treatment and ultimately a cure, and will support any organization that is fighting for that same goal.

It has only been a little over a year since Grant was diagnosed. The news has not stolen my happiness, but it has definitely added a dark threatening cloud into my life that never goes away. I still love my life, my husband, and my children. I look forward to all the same things I did before: trick-or-treating on Halloween, opening gifts Christmas morning, and a night out with good friends. I do not believe I will ever be able to say this disease has made me appreciate my life any more. I loved my life just the way it was. I was very lucky. The disease, though, has changed the focus of my life. I am still learning how to turn this negative focal point into something positive for Grant and my family. It is very difficult. As you read through this book, you are sure to find stories of inspiration from many of the older boys and young men living with Duchenne. I hope to raise Grant to have that same kind of hope, determination, and purpose that many of them have shared with me. That is what is important. Many people waste their lives away to drugs, alcoholism, self-inflicted drama, or just pure laziness. These people have a choice in life and choose to waste it. They may have hardships to overcome, but not impossibilities. Duchenne is still an impossibility waiting to be defeated. Grant does not have a choice in his disease, but we as a family have a choice in how we think about it, how we talk about it, and how we live every day. For him, we will make the best of this impossible, unimaginable situation and teach him that each day is what you make of it. The small things in life do matter and everyone has the opportunity to make a difference.

Heather Kessler Meermann
Grant's Mommy

Warrick, 5 Years Old

Feeling God's comfort in Duchenne

Our son Warrick was diagnosed with Duchenne Muscular Dystrophy (DMD) at 5 years old, after 4 years of routine blood tests and 1 liver biopsy to try to figure out why he had what we thought were elevated liver enzymes. By chance, we found out his enzymes were elevated when he was 1. He was running a fever for a few days with no other symptoms, so his pediatrician ran blood work to see if he had an infection. Turns out he just had Roseola, a common childhood illness, but in this blood work the doctor noticed that Warrick's AST and ALT enzymes were extremely highly elevated, so he referred us to a pediatric gastrointestinal specialist. In addition to this, Warrick seemed a little like a late bloomer when it came to walking. I would say he was finally an 'official' walker at 15 months old. In our Mommy & Me classes, I also noticed that Warrick wasn't able to get up off of the floor from the middle of the room like his peers could. He always had to crawl to someone or something to help him pull himself up. He also fell down quite a bit. So much in fact, he would fall and automatically call out, "I'm okay!" that it had become such a normal thing to us. We took notice of these things; however, from reading different parenting books and talking to our own friends and family, we went with that thing they say about not comparing your child to others. Every child develops at their own pace, blah, blah, so we just went with it. Oh, and did I tell you about this kid's calf muscles?! They were huge! He was so muscular. We loved our little muscle man and his big ol' calf muscles. We always thought it was so cool. Little did we know.

When baby brother Ryker arrived, we started noticing so many things that Ryker did as an infant and toddler that Warrick hadn't ever done. All the while, his falling down was happening more and more. We also started experiencing some behavioral and emotional struggles with him that at times were overwhelming on their own. I mentioned this to his pediatrician a couple of times as well. I had always kept him up to date on the monitoring we were still doing regarding his elevated enzymes. Warrick was about 4 1/2 now, so his pediatrician decided to send us for a second opinion regarding the elevated enzymes because we should have had an answer by now. At our first appointment with Warrick's new pediatric GI specialist, I remember him mentioning that he was concerned about the pediatrician notes stating that Warrick was falling down a lot. But since we were referred to him for a "liver' issue, he told us he would run the usual blood tests and do a second liver biopsy just to see if it was, in fact, a liver issue. And just as they had for the previous 4 years, all liver tests came back inconclusive, showing no problem with the liver. At our follow up for the second biopsy, the doctor broke it to us that he did not think it was a liver issue, but that the elevated enzyme levels, combined with the falling down that we had been concerned about, looked more like it might be muscular dystrophy. He asked us if Warrick had trouble getting up off of the ground to stand up. We said, "Well, he can do it, but this is what he does," and my husband proceeded to show the doctor how we often saw Warrick get to his feet. I was surprised when the doctor shared with us that this way of getting up has its own name--The Gowers' Sign.

When I heard muscular dystrophy, I didn't know too much about it, but I remember associating a wheelchair to the disease. With that visual, I took it in for a minute and said to myself ,"Ok, so he may end up in a wheelchair at some point down the line when he's older. Ok, we can do this. At least he is going to be OK." Or so I thought. The doctor also said the word Duchenne several times and Becker maybe once or twice. Since it is not his field, he was hesitant to give us too much information on the disease and whether he was sure it was Duchenne or Becker. To be honest, I am a little grateful that I didn't know too much about the disease at that moment, because I probably would have freaked out and lost it right there in the room in front of the doctor, my husband and children. When I got home and started looking it up online, I just cried and prayed to God that it wasn't so--and that if it was, that it wouldn't be Duchenne. Not that Becker is any less devastating, but at the moment it seemed the less grim of the two. But I knew in my gut, all signs pointed to Duchenne. The doctor ordered a blood test to find out Warrick's creatine kinase (CK) level and informed us that, depending on the results of this, it could let us know if we were looking at muscular dystrophy or not. A normal range for a CK level is 22 to 198 U/L (units per liter). For the longest 48 hours of our lives, we waited to get the results of this blood test. Finally, the doctor called an informed me that Warrick's CK level was elevated above 10,000. We were immediately referred to an MD clinic with a neurologist, who officially diagnosed Warrick with Duchenne Muscular Dystrophy.

On one hand, I truly feel like I can say that this all came out of left field and it was utterly shocking, but on the other hand, we had known for a while that there was "something" going on with our son. We just never, EVER, thought it was something as devastating as DMD. Once we researched the disease and read more about it, it was clear that Warrick had been showing many symptoms of DMD for a long time, but with no family history of the disease and no reason to ever look for it, we had no idea. We started him on a daily steroid treatment immediately. This has, so far, helped keep him from falling down so much, hardly at all now. He can run a little better, pedal a bike more easily. It's been nice to see him not struggle with these things so much anymore. The falling down had started getting serious. Before he was diagnosed, he had fallen down some cement steps at our church and his face was really scraped up, like road rash. Two weeks before his diagnosis, he got his first set of stitches on his head, because he was attempting to run to the couch, and just as he got to it he fell and cracked his head on the corner frame of the couch. It's scary to think of what else could have happened to him had his diagnosis come any later. As of now, we are just a few months into this life with Duchenne. Warrick is still very active, running and playing all day long. If you didn't know any better, you wouldn't even know he had this nasty disease in his precious body. He seems perfect in every way, looking from the outside.

So, now that I've shared a little of our journey to our life with DMD, which is an ugly, cruel, sad, dark, heartbreaking world at times, it's on my heart to share how, amidst all of the bad that this disease has brought into our lives, I've been able to know God's comfort through it all and have had some really special moments.

Here goes. My father, with whom I had a close and special father-daughter relationship, passed away when I was 19 years old. Sadly, he and my children never had a chance to know each other. A month or so after Warrick's diagnosis, I came across an old newspaper clipping from something I definitely had memories of from my childhood. I was brought to tears as I read it again for the first time in a long time. In the summer of 1985, when I was 7 years old, my Dad, along with 7 other of his friends, did a charity ride on 10-speed bikes from a 7-Eleven store in Tustin, California, to Las Vegas, Nevada, 372 miles. Their team raised over $3,000 for this event. The charity he did this for was for the MDA and Jerry's Kids. It was such a comforting thing for me, in that moment, to know that my Dad had done something so selfless while he was alive that would one day help his first born grandchild in his fight against this disease, and he had no way of knowing he would be a part of this fight for his grandson, yet he is. I love and miss my Dad so much. He was always so good with kids, I know he would have loved being a Grandpa, and I wish my kids could have known him. But for these things to come together in this way was such a blessing to me. I know it was God comforting me.

My Grams also passed away, 1 year before we got Warrick's diagnosis. She and I were very close and she loved both of my boys so much. They were both a big part of her inspiration to fight so hard and for so long against the cancer she had. One of the first thoughts I had after we found out about the DMD was that I was grateful that my grandma didn't have to know that

Warrick had this disease. It would have broken her heart. After she passed away, I was searching for the perfect music to put with a beautiful picture slide show of her. I came across the song "Smile" by Nat King Cole, and after listening to it and reading the lyrics, I felt it was perfect for my Grams. So a year later, after my son's diagnosis, when the time came for the MDA Jerry Lewis Telethon to air, I was reading up on it online and came across a section that highlighted the history of the theme song of the telethon. It noted, "Since the show's inception, its theme has been 'Smile.'" That song really touched my heart when I picked it for my Grams and I came to love it very much and listen to it often since she died. Then again, something from this disease was linked with something completely separate in my life, and I just felt that it was God, comforting me again.

Since Warrick is only 5 years old, we have only shared age-appropriate truth and details with him regarding this disease he is living with. Obviously, he's aware that he was falling down a lot, had trouble running, pedaling, jumping and would get tired easily, even from walking short distances. So we've been able to share with him that his muscles need a little more rest than some other people. He knows he has to take his steroid medicine daily to help keep his muscles strong. When we've done fundraisers, we explained to him that we were raising money to give to the doctors so that they can find a way to keep his muscles strong all of the time and hopefully stop him having to take medicine every day. I was a little disturbed at first when, on his own, out of the blue one day, Warrick was pretending to be in a wheel-chair, and started talking to me about when he would be in a wheelchair some day. It scared me. I wondered if he overheard some conversation about that part of the disease, since we haven't shared those sort of details with him yet. I asked him why he thought he would be in a wheelchair some day and he simply answered, "Because sometimes peoples legs just don't work and they have to be in a wheelchair." I asked him how he knew that and he said, "Because on [the cartoon] Little Bill, his friend was in a wheelchair, and I thought it looked neat. I think I would like to be in one." And this, too, was somehow comforting for me. Not because I want him to be in a wheelchair, or am OK with him being in one, or because I will ever give up fighting for him to NOT have to be in one, but because he would be ok with it. Even though he doesn't even know that part of the disease he is living with, at his young and innocent age, he is accepting that sometimes, "people's legs just don't work," as he put it, and they have to be in wheelchairs. Again, I feel this is God's comfort over us. He knows us personally, each and everyone, inside and out. He knows specifically just what to do to get each individual person's attention to remind and show us he is always with us, comforting, loving and teaching us, even through our darkest experiences in life. My hope and prayer is for all families fighting this disease together to be be able to know the same comfort I have. It's there. You just have to be willing to look for it, and you will see it!!

As for me and our family - we are Warrick's Warriors and Warriors for everyone suffering from this disease and WE WILL END DUCHENNE!!

Be joyful in hope, patient in affliction, faithful in prayer. Romans12:12.

Leigh Pernosky

Hunter, 7 Years Old

When my son, Hunter, was eighteen months old, he wasn't quite walking yet. My brother, Allen, had Duchenne Muscular Dystrophy, but the DNA test I took before I was pregnant with my oldest daughter came back negative and I was told I only had a 6 percent chance of having a son with DMD. Having a brother with Duchenne was a painful childhood memory. Allen, who was four years older than I, died when he was 28 years old. The last seven years of his life were spent bedridden.

My mother suggested I test Hunter for DMD, to rule it out completely, and our pediatrician agreed it would be a good idea. The first, quickest test was to check his ck blood level. It came back as high, which could mean a few things, DMD included. He then had the same DNA test that I took. It came back negative, but because of his high ck level, they took his DNA and went through each gene. They found 1 gene affected,which meant yes, he has Duchenne Muscular Dystrophy.

My worst nightmare had just come true. I think growing up knowing about this disease made this diagnosis even harder. The doctor tried to tell me about new treatments, trials and what to expect. I did not want (at first) to hear any of it. I had watched as my brother had gone from braces, to a wheelchair, to being bedridden. I had seen the toll it had taken on my parents and their relationship. I also saw how strong they were and I didn't feel that I could be that strong.

I crawled up in my bed and cried like I never had before. My mother came to me. I told her I didn't know what to do or how I could even deal with this. My mother said that my children needed me, Hunter needed me and that I just needed to take things day by day and just take care of my kids like I always do. It was hard but I did. A few weeks later I learned I was pregnant. I was more scared than ever, but after more testing, the doctors concluded I was having a girl and I wouldn't have to worry about her having DMD. My daughters, Brittany and Caitlyn, have been a blessing to our family and to Hunter. They really keep him moving and help him stay strong.

Hunter is now seven years old. He goes to public school. He goes to physical therapy twice a week and wears braces at night. When he feels week, he adjusts. When he asks why, his dad and I tell him the best way we can. He is an incredible boy with a big, bright smile.

I still sit on my bed and cry sometimes. When Hunter has trouble getting up from the floor, trouble on the stairs, or leg cramps my heart breaks, but then I see that smile of his and I know I must stay strong. Every morning when he comes down the stairs on his own is a good day. We are actively involved in spreading awareness of this disease and we raise money for research.

Each day is a different challenge for us, but we are very hopeful and we are coping the best way we know how, for Hunter.

Brenda Burk-mom of three wonderful children

Kelvin, 8 Years Old

No one can imagine the shock experienced when you are told that your child has a fatal disease, no one, except a parent that has received such horrible news about their child. The shock delivered the worst pain, both physically and mentally, that I'd ever experienced. This happened to me when a doctor at our children's hospital told me that my son had Duchenne Muscular Dystrophy. No one had told me that I should bring my husband Henry with me, so I was alone with the doctor, while my son Kelvin was with a nurse in the next room. The doctor left the exam room only a few minutes after telling me about Kelvin. I started to cry like I've never cried before. These are tears that make your heart feel like it is ready to explode. I was so thankful that the most wonderful nurse came into the room and knelt down and prayed with me. The date was January 9, 2008. Kelvin was five years old.

I knew from the time Kelvin was born that he seemed different, at least much different from his older sister Malia. He was born three weeks and one day early but was very healthy and weighed 7lb 10oz. Kelvin immediately struggled with nursing. He couldn't breast feed, and after trying about eight different bottle nipples, he was finally able to nurse.

Kelvin did well during his first year of life. He met all of the milestones and then started walking at 12 months of age. This is when I started to recognize that there might be something wrong. Even though he was walking, he fell constantly. He always had huge bumps and bruises on his head, lip, and knees. Kelvin would fall while walking straight; however, the doctor said he was still learning. Kelvin also drooled constantly, way beyond anything that I've ever seen.

Over the next few years, Kelvin begged to be carried everywhere we went and he would bend over and rub his thighs and say that his legs hurt. At that time, I still felt something was wrong, but every time I'd tell his doctor, he'd check him out and tell me that it was just growing pains. Other adults would tell us that Kelvin knew how to use us by getting us to carry him. I felt that I must be wrong about Kelvin and I started to believe his doctor and what other folks were saying.

After Kelvin turned three, he improved, or, well, we thought he did. He fell very little and wasn't tired after walking a lot. However, I started to notice other things that didn't seem right. He couldn't hold crayons properly and couldn't color like other children. Kelvin couldn't jump across a line or even a pencil. He would look like he was skipping or galloping when he'd try to jump. He started having terrible tantrums. He couldn't run as fast as other boys, but he was shorter, so there always appeared to be an explanation.

When Kelvin turned four, we entered him in a local church sponsored preschool. The teachers there noticed that he couldn't manage writing skills very well and appeared to have fine motor skill problems. The school sent an informational sheet about a free county screening for children who might need to be tested for developmental disabilities. Once again, I thought I'd try to find out what could be wrong. Kelvin went through a variety of tests: vision, hearing, lead poisoning, gross motor skills, fine motor skills, cognitive skills, etc. The folks reviewed the results immediately and did have concern for his gross motor skills, fine motor skills, and cognitive delay. We were then referred to the county preschool that has programs to help children that need assistance in order to enter kindergarten. We only have one county preschool that receives federal funds so that children can receive proper help, no matter what their family income may be. It is in a town about 20 miles from our house.

Kelvin entered the new preschool and had teachers who were college ed-ucated and were qualified to assist children with many different developmental disabilities. Kelvin thrived; however, I still had concern. His physical therapist at the preschool also noted that Kelvin had very large calves. Of course, we later found out that this is one of the signs of Duchenne Muscular Dystrophy.

During Kelvin's fifth year doctor appointment, I once again talked to his doctor about my concerns. The doctor checked over everything again and was ready to send us on our way. I got upset and refused to leave the room unless he would order either blood tests or x-rays to see what could be wrong. The doctor then took time to review information that his preschool physical therapist had written as well as documented information from my past concerns that were in his chart. The doctor wrote a prescription for x-rays and set up a follow-up appointment with a top orthopedic doctor.

After a few weeks, we went to the orthopedic doctor. He reviewed the x-rays and didn't see anything. He had Kelvin sit on the floor and get up fast. Then he had him climb onto the exam table. The doctor discussed three conditions that he thought Kelvin might have. He said Kelvin was either slow to progress and that he would catch up, that Kelvin had Leukemia or that he had Muscular Dystrophy, but, that he was 95% sure that it wasn't Muscular Dystrophy. He said that he would go ahead and run some blood tests, but not to worry about it.

After a few more weeks, we received a call and were told that we had an appointment set up with a physical medicine doctor at our local children's hospital. This is where our nightmare began. What I thought was going to be an appointment to just take another look at Kelvin turned into complete and utter devastation. I really couldn't believe what I was being told, but it finally confirmed that I had been correct for five years and that something was wrong. However, I had never dreamed that it could be something as serious and fatal as Duchenne Muscular Dystrophy. After crying and going into shock and praying with the nurse, the doctor then told me that he'd be the doctor that I'd see when my son needed braces, a scooter or a wheelchair. Can you imagine? The doctor had just told me that my son may not live past age 20 and he immediately went to talking about a wheelchair. How could this be possible? I had a beautiful five-year-old little boy, who would soon lose his ability to walk, feed himself, and die at a young age. I couldn't believe it; however, this is when our new life began. We've never looked back and as you can imagine, we will never visit that doctor again.

Our new life consisted of finding out everything that we could to help Kelvin. My family and friends researched online for thousands of hours. We read about supplements, steroids, braces, doctors, our son's deletion, the lack of a treatment or a cure, etc., and soon we were on our way to dealing with Duchenne Muscular Dystrophy the best way that we knew how. We also had to get over the guilt that we had for not figuring this out sooner and for pushing Kelvin to walk, climb, and run when he was younger. We started networking with people that we met at doctor visits and especially online through Parent Project Muscular Dystrophy, where there is a lot of information and discussions written by parents of children with Duchenne Muscular Dystrophy. We now network through Facebook, too, which has been amazing. I have a network of "friends" around the entire world. I love every one of them and could never have survived without them. It is the network of support that helps keep all of us determined that there will be an end to Duchenne Muscular Dystrophy. The parents with whom I've networked most are those willing to go to any length to help their children, even losing their homes and their jobs, whatever it takes. We'll travel to get to the best doctors anywhere in the world and will pay out-of-pocket for unpaid medical expenses,if needed. All that matters is caring as best as we can for our sons. And until there is a treatment or cure, we will do everything humanly possible to keep them healthier, in hopes that they'll have help soon.

Duchenne Muscular Dystrophy has been both the worst and best thing that has ever happened to me. I have been through three years full of ups and downs, but I have become a better person and now understand how parents suffer when they can't help their children. I am appreciative of little things in life and don't care about material things for myself. I used to plan for the future by saving for my retirement and for my children's education: however, now we don't want to, nor do we have time to think about the future. We are spending more time and often more money, to enjoy doing all that we can with our children today. This disease has shown me that we should all be living for today anyway, as our time here on earth is uncertain for all of us.

Unfortunately, I am reminded daily of what we are dealing with through everything that I have to do, but also by simple words that other parents never have to think of. The simple words I'm referring to are, "When I grow up..." For the first five years of Kelvin's life, it never occurred to me that these words could bring so many tears and heartache. For many parents these simple words bring joy, listening to ideas that their children have about what they may do some day. To a parent with a child with Duchenne Muscular Dystrophy, they bring a fear of tomorrow, not knowing if a treatment or cure will come in time for them. Kelvin uses these words often and I can only pray that his words and wishes do come true.

Until you've had to deal with something like this, curled up in shock in a fetal position, there is no way that you can say that you understand how it feels. It is impossible. I don't mean anything negative by this statement. It is the truth. It is so easy for us to say that we understand. I know that I have. People who care can support you, be there for you, advocate for you, listen to you, donate to organizations that are working to keep our children walking and alive and lend a hand to parents, because many things no longer get finished that you used to have time for. Dealing with doctor appointments, buying supplements, buying steroids from England, massaging, stretching, putting on braces, dealing with schooling issues, dental issues, reduced sodium diets, etc. take a lot of our time and many things in our every day lives aren't as important any longer, even though they still need to be done. Our boys are our lives, and that is it.

Everyone has something serious or a cause that they have to deal with in life and ours ended up being Duchenne Muscular Dystrophy. When we found out about Kelvin, my family decided immediately that we'd live life to the fullest through our faith and take one day at a time. We have done just that.

This is our life, this is our journey, this is our cause. Our journey won't end until every boy born with Duchenne Muscular Dystrophy can live a life without the pain, symptoms or death caused from this terrible disease. We know that we can end Duchenne, if we continue forward with one voice, together.

We are so thankful to everyone who has been part of our journey.

Michelle L Jones

Brandon, 8 Years Old

A Blessing Named Brandon

On a beautiful February morning of 2004, my husband, Bobby; six-year-old daughter, Amber; and myself welcomed 19-month-old Brandon Lee Hathaway into our home after a long wait of almost two years. You see, Brandon was the second of our now three adopted children from our local Department of Social Services (DSS) here in South Carolina. His red hair, baby blue eyes and beautiful smile lit up our lives from the very moment we laid eyes on him.

In the beginning, we knew that Brandon had some developmental delays due to the lack of experience and stimulation he had encountered during his time in foster care. We were very concerned about him and had addressed these delays through physical, speech and occupational therapy, but nothing had prepared us for the most devastating day of our lives.....October 22, 2008. The day Brandon was diagnosed with Duchenne Muscular Dystrophy (DMD), a progressive muscle disease that to date has no treatment or cure. It was a day we'll never forget...one that changed our lives forever. We immediately called our family from N.C., our closest friends, and our church family asking for prayer and wisdom as to how we were going to handle this disease and how, or if, we were going to tell Brandon and his siblings.

We contacted our local MDA office and met with Rachel, whom we now call "our girl," and wereon our way to becoming a part of a new family....The Duchenne Community.

Over the past two years we have been very proactive in raising money and awareness for this disease through bake sales, Defeat Duchenne, a 5k run hosted by our church, Standing Springs Baptist, a letter writing campaign, and have partnered with local businesses and restaurants willing to host events in honor of our son. We have absolutely been overwhelmed with the outpouring support of our family, friends, church, and community and have met amazing people from across the globe. We feel so blessed to be connected with the best researchers, doctors and therapists who specialize in DMD and are so thankful to have this opportunity to share our story. Our faith in God has grown by leaps and bounds as we know He is the only way we have gotten through this journey thus far along with our amazing family and literally hundreds of prayer warriors from around the world who pray for our family regularly. God's word tells us in Jeremiah 33:3, "Call to me and I will tell you great and mighty things you do not know." We may not know what the future holds but what we do know is that He is a healing God who performs miracles each and everyday.

Words can't express how blessed we were back in February of 2004 when Brandon was placed in our lives. God knew that Brandon needed us and that we needed him! He is now in second grade and thriving in every way. He loves bugs, swimming, video games, art, being a cub scout and playing with his brother, Ethan, who is 3, and sister, Amber, who is 12. He wears his AFO's (he calls them Spider Man boots) each night, takes his steroid, deflazacort, which we get from Canada, and CoQ10, a supplement, each day like a champ. He sees a physical therapist every six weeks and his dynamic comprehensive care management team twice a year at Cincinatti's Children's Hospital. I honestly don't know what we would do without the guidance of Dr. Wong, Dr. Rybalsky and her amazing team. They, along, with Pat Furlong, founder of Parent Project Muscular Dystrophy (PPMD), have been so inspirational, supportive, and available to us on a whim, even though we are miles apart. We had no idea this was the path we would be taking in our lives, but God knew and that's all that matters. "You chart the path ahead of me and tell me where to stop and rest. Every moment you know where I am." Psalm 139:3. Please feel free to contact me at lynnlee@charter.net if you would like to be on our prayer warrior list and/or would like to talk about your experiences. We've had so many caring supporters over the past two years, and we'd love to be able to give back. In closing, I would like to say I love you to my precious parents, Linda and Melvin Hicks, my wonderful sister, Alison Bradley and family, my awesome brother, Melvin Hicks, Jr. and family and to my husband's loving parents, Bob and Shirley Hathaway. Also to my extended family for their love and support, my dear friends, my school, Mauldin Elementary , my church, and last but not least, my loving husband, Bobby, and three angels, Amber, Brandon and Ethan. I love you all to the sky and back and as far as numbers can go! Continue keeping us in prayer as we move forward in putting an end to Duchenne.

Joyful blessings,Julie Hathaway

Brayden, 7 Years Old

Not a good April's Fools Day.

April 1ˢᵗ, 2010, a day of jokes and pranks. This was not a funny day for our family. This was the day our world was turned upside down.

It all started with a 3-month checkup for Brayden's ADHD medicine. I asked Dr. Joe to take a look at some other concerns that I have had since Brayden was 2 years old. He did not run like other kids his age and had always had a very hard time getting off the floor from a sitting position. He would struggle getting up and he would try to get up butt first. So the doctor did some field test and then decided to do some blood work and then also send him for a bilateral hip x-ray. He said that he wanted to rule out anything going on in his hips, such as leukemia. Of course, I agreed.

A week went by and finally on March 29ᵗʰ, 2010, Dr. Joe's nurse called me at work and said that the results were in and that the doctor wanted to see David and me in his office that day. At that moment, my heart sank. I asked if everything was ok, and she said that Dr. Joe wanted Brayden to see a specialist. I immediately thought oncologist, orthopedist. I NEVER dreamed of what was around the corner...

As we drove to the doctor's office, David and I hardly said a word. We had no clue what we were about to be told. We just knew it was something NOT good. When we walked into the office, we were asked to have a seat in the waiting room and were told that Dr. Joe would be in shortly. David and I sat in the empty waiting room for what seemed like FOREVER. Dr. Joe waited until his last patient had gone for the day and came in sat down and shut the door. Now, Dr. Joe is usually all smiles but when he walked in, there was this look of sorrow. He sat down and said, "Well, the results are in and I had some concerns about some enzyme levels. I have already consulted with a neurologist and between what the tests show and her expertise, we believe that Brayden has some form of muscular dystrophy. "

Now, I knew what MD was. As a mother, my heart just shattered into a million pieces. I knew that there was no cure and that I was going to have to just sit and watch my child DIE! David, on the other hand, had no clue what we were dealing with. After lots of questions and emotions running high, Dr. Joe told us that he was very sorry and that if there was anything that he could do, would we please let him know. He also told me as we were leaving that the neurologist would be getting in touch with us and that she could see Brayden that same week. I said thank you and David and I went to the car. We just sat there in complete silence. Neither one of us knew what to say to the other. Then, as if on cue, we both burst into tears and asked, "WHY?"'

On the way home there was silence in the car. We both were in shock. The drive that only takes 30 minutes seemed to take hours. I just knew that when I walked through the front door and saw Brayden, I might not be able to hold it together. We pulled into the drive way and neither of us could get out. Finally, I got out because I knew that if I didn't, the kids would be out in a flash. David sat in the car for a few more minutes to try to gather his thoughts. I walked in and saw Brayden Bop and hugged him and cried like a baby. He had no clue why I was sobbing. He just wanted to try to make it better. I then had to break the news to my mom (Granna) that her only grandson had some form of muscular dystrophy. As I was taking her into the other room, I saw Brayden run out the front door after his daddy, and he caught his father crying like a baby. Our world was devastated.

A few days had passed, but reality still had not sunk in all the way. This was April 1st, 2010, D-day. We headed out to Atlanta to the neurologist and this was the 1st day that Brayden had missed school since starting Pre-K. As we got closer, the knot in my stomach grew bigger and bigger. We finally arrived and went upstairs, checked in and waited for his name to be called. My heart was racing. "Brayden Eubanks," we heard. This time my heart was in my throat. We met Dr. Joann Janas, the neurologist. She introduced herself to us and then started talking to us. Then finally, she gave us her evaluation. When that part was over, she concluded that he had Duchenne. Although I knew what MD was, I didn't know what Duchenne was, but I had a feeling that I was about to find out. She then explained it to us. Then told us what we could expect, but she was unsure of how progressive it would be for him, that it is different for everyone. One part that got me was that she told us that he could be in a wheelchair as soon as age 8-12. He is 7 NOW. I was sick to my stomach, and all I could think about was how I was going to tell him what was going on and what to say when things started progressing. Lord only knows. But Dr. Janas advised us that because he didn't know something was wrong, there was no reason to tell him what was to come. We would tell him that something was wrong with his muscles and that we were going to do whatever we could to make them healthier. As the appointment went on, she explained to us that we needed to get a genetic test done to see if Brayden has duplication or a deletion. After four weeks of waiting, the results came in and showed that he has a deletion of exons 3-11. All that meant to us was that there are NO TRIALS for his deletion. Then she advised me to get tested to see if I am a carrier since there is no history of MD in our family. NOW all I could think was, if I am, then what if my 2-year-old daughter is, also? Well, only time will tell.

A few months have gone by at this point and the shock factor has worn off. I still have breakdowns here and there, but not like before. David and I have accepted it and will move on and live every day to the fullest. You have to accept it or it will eat you alive inside. This is what God has given us, and we will deal with it the best we can. Brayden has a very "normal" life. He is still able to play baseball, which he LOVES, run to an extent, and can do almost anything he wants to, except for strength training.

After the shock and heartbreak, I turned to the MDA website. That is where I had made a profile because I needed to be able to talk about it with other parents because I didn't have a support group. So from there, I decided to look on Facebook to see what other organizations were out there for DMD support. That is where I knew that I was at home with this, that there were other families out there like us, just finding out when their child was 6 or 7. And then there were others who had been dealing with this for years. I knew that there was HOPE. That is also when Misty Vanderweele reached out to me, and ever since then, as my husband says, "She is like a celebrity in the Eubanks' house." She and her family have given David and me hope. I have a warm feeling about this that everything is going to be all right.

As we kept up with Misty and Luke, her son, we noticed that she was doing this massive packing for Texas. So one day I asked her why she was going to Texas all the way from Alaska. She told us about this doctor there twho was treating kids with DMD and gave me the website. I immediately looked at it and I knew that Brayden HAD to go there.

Time went on and we were going to PT and stretching Brayden, when we decided we were going to do whatever we had to do to get him to Corpus Christi, Texas. In a matter of 3 weeks we had raised over $10,000 for what we needed to get him there. That was the best feeling in the world. THANK YOU MISTY VANDERWEELE.

If you find out when your child is 2 or when he is 7 that he has Duchenne, his age doesn't make a difference because there is always the doubt in the back of your mind that there will ever be a cure. But with today's technology, there is this little thing called HOPE, and we have IT!

Deni Eubanks

Levi, 7 Years Old

Our life was beyond perfect. That is until Christmas Eve 2008. That's the day our life ended as we knew it and changed into this intense journey of heartache, profound sadness, tears heavier than raindrops, joy, prayer and, most of all, hope.

Levi is our 3rd son and is the funniest little guy around. His big brown eyes captivate all whom he meets, and then he blurts out his infamous saying, "Hey, Good Looking." You can't help but melt. Levi has 2 older brothers, Luke & Lance, who adore him. Levi had some slight developmental delays as an infant, so we had a physical therapist come to our home. She got him to walk at 18 months. Our pediatrician wasn't too concerned because all children develop differently.

How wrong we were!

I wanted to get one more PT session in before the holiday, so I scheduled it on Xmas Eve. I told the PT that Levi did this very cute and funny thing, he put his hands on his knees when trying to stand up. She knew it was anything but cute and funny. What Levi was doing was called "gowering," which is indicative of what would forever change our lives.

She said a 2-year-old should not be gowering and then, on Xmas Eve, she uttered the words that resonate so crisply and clearly even today, "I think Levi has muscular dystrophy." How did we get here? She was just coming for a brief PT session, I thought exercises were in store…How wrong I was!

My husband and I decided to keep this to ourselves as it was Xmas Eve. How were we going to get through the holidays? Excruciating doesn't even describe the pain. The day after Xmas, we told our parents that Levi was going for tests. I didn't dare mention MD. They put on a brave face but they knew something wasn't right.

A simple blood test confirmed the unthinkable. But they mentioned this strange word-- "Duchenne." What on God's earth was that? Our hearts were heavy; how could this be? A few days before, we were laughing at Levi because he was a clumsy 2-year-old, and now that clumsiness had a deadly name, Duchenne. **How wrong we were!**

Since the diagnosis almost 2 years ago, we have changed! We look at life differently. We try to keep the normalcy for our boys, but IT always weighs heavily on our souls. We have learned through research, faith and hope that better things are coming for Levi and all the boys with Duchenne.

It may not be the life we dreamed of for our beautiful boy, but it will be one filled with tremendous love and hope for a happy future.

How Right I am !

Levi's MomPerlita

Cade, 8 Years Old

<u>C</u>rusade <u>A</u>gainst <u>D</u>uchenne <u>E</u>mpowerment

 Cade is my angel! He is a true blessing sent from Heaven. Born ten weeks early, he came out fighting for his life and continues to fight on a daily basis. On Cade's sixth birthday, he was diagnosed with Duchenne's Muscular Dystrophy. It changed our world forever. It was a devastating diagnosis that took our family on a roller coaster ride. This is how our journey began four years .....

Cade was always a step behind since birth. We took him to many doctors who diagnosed him as deaf, autistic, speech impaired, and mentally disabled. We were even told by some doctors that this was normal for a "premie," and he would eventually catch up. Honestly, after each test failed, I began to think I was crazy or just overreacting as a first time mom. I felt relieved when the doctors said "nothing" was wrong, but deep down in my heart I knew something was just not right. When Cade started preschool at the age of four, his teacher suggested that he have physical therapy. I realized that I was not crazy and that now we could get my boy the help he needed to catch up. Then we could finally move on with our lives. After a year, the physical therapist suggested that he see a neurologist because she believed he might have a neuromuscular disorder. Now I know I can be very hard headed and a little out of line sometimes, but I told that therapist very rudely that she was crazy and that my son did not have such a thing! I left her office very sad, frustrated, angry, and wanted to fight anyone who crossed my path. I went home, talked to my family, calmed down, and began searching the Internet for answers. As a suggestion, never do this! I found hundreds of possible things that it could be. I related every symptom to Cade. I realized that this was more serious than I had first thought. So against it all, I contacted a well known pediatric specialist and the first available appointment was not for a year. "Are you kidding me?" Needless to say, it was a very long wait.

May 3, 2008, was the day of our first appointment. The pediatric specialist went over a few tests and surveys and quickly ruled out autism. She noticed that his heels cords were really tight, so he needed to stay in therapy. She was not sure of the problem, but would run a panel of blood tests to get to the bottom of it. She briefly mentioned a test for the neuromuscular disorder MD, but was positive that that was not the problem. I left her office a bundle of nerves and waited for the dreaded phone call. Two days later, the pediatric specialist called and told me that Cade's CPK was 18,000, which was an indication of a neuromuscular disorder. This changed our lives forever. We had to go back on May 8th to get genetic testing done on Cade, which would take six weeks to get the results. Within those six weeks, I realized something major was wrong. Once again I caught myself researching the Internet to come up with my own conclusions. The Internet is a wonderful thing; however, I believe that a worried parent should never try to diagnose their own child. June 18, 2008, Cade's sixth birthday, we went to the clinic and were told very rudely that our child had Duchenne Muscular Dystrophy. I was full of emotions. I was angry for this to be happening to our family, but yet relieved at the same time that I finally had an answer. My next question was, "How do we fix it?" When I realized this was a life-threatening disease without a cure that affects all his muscles, I was crushed like someone was ripping my heart out of my chest. I questioned my belief in God, my own life, and asked, "Why me?" I quickly realized that I had to be strong and fight for my son's life. So together our family fought, together we learned, and together we are beating the odds of DMD and raising awareness. I believe God has sent me a gift and I truly believe that it is my duty on Earth to find my angel a cure to give him a life that he deserves.

Cade is now eight years old and in the 2nd Grade. We start our day at 7:30 am with medicines, then breakfast, and off to school. Cade has an IEP at school in which he receives OT, PT, and speech. At 3:30 he returns home from school, eats supper, completes homework, plays on the computer, bathes, and goes to bed with nighttime AFO's (leg braces) to prevent contractors. Our life outside, looking in, seems pretty normal, but this is so far from reality. Our life has consisted of many medical doctors and professionals that offer our son no hope. The only available treatment thus far is steroids, so I made the bold decision to give him these to treat DMD. The neurologists told us a little bit about the side effects of steroids, but at the time I honestly didn't listen. All I really heard is that the steroids will keep him walking longer and protect his heart and lungs, which sounded convincing to me. As a mother, I feel at the time I made the best choice for Cade. Two years later, I am not so sure. I feel, initially, I made the choice for me. Besides gaining weight, not growing, and depleting bone density, Cade is not happy. He went from being a happy child with no worries to a child who has violent outrages on a daily basis. Yes, he still walks, but is that fair for him or me? There came a time in my life about two months ago that I realized that "I" am afraid of the wheelchair. This drug helps me to keep Cade looking so-called "normal." I am in the process of decreasing his steroids. Right or wrong, I will no longer sit back and watch these drugs take over his body. I will no longer sacrifice his quality of life. I honestly believe that if Cade is walking and appears "normal," then I can prevail into a fantasy land where nothing is wrong. Reality soon sets in as I watch him not be able to keep up with his peers on a daily basis. As a mother, it is our job to protect and cure illness from our children, but with DMD, my hands are tied. I am not in control.

As a parent advocate, I will no longer sit back and have no hope. I am researching and doing fundraisers, all in attempt to one day find a cure not only for Cade, but all boys affected by DMD. I believe we are close in our crusade. I recently visited Dr. Rhodes in Texas and I have never met a person or doctor like him. He sat with us at his office and spoke with us for three hours, like Cade was his own child. He brought a whole new explanation of DMD and opened our eyes to new possibilities. He gave our family back hope. After one week on the STS treatment, Cade is running like he never ran before and is happy. He has lots of energy. His coordination has improved so that he can stand on one foot, which was impossible a week ago. This may seem small to some, but for a child with DMD, this is huge. He walks for several hours without getting tired, whereas before, he was tired after fifteen minutes. Now I am a skeptic, but "seeing is believing!" Cade has suffered from headaches and back pain for two years and almost instantly was relieved of these pains. He did not complain about these issues the whole week in Texas. This may be the answer that our DMD community has been looking for and only time will tell. We will fight the power that DMD has over the bodies of our children and create the empowerment our children deserve!

Overall, to sum up our lives over the past four years, I would not change a thing! Although it has not been an easy path, I believe I have learned to look at life in a new light. Each day is a blessing, and I am so proud of the accomplishment my son has made. Everyone has to deal with life situations, and sometimes the road may not be easy for everyone. Faith may even get broken, but there is hope for a better future if we just believe. We cannot choose the cards that we are dealt; however, we do have our own voice to challenge them. I must live in the present and not worry so much about the future. I thank my past for making the building blocks that has led me to the strong-willed person I am today. I now have hope and faith that God will help me through the troubled waters with the support of family and friends. Cade and I can get through anything that tries to challenge our well being. God bless the broken road that led me on this heartfelt journey in the life of DMD. My hope is that in my child's lifetime, we can look at DMD as a thing of the past. All our children deserve a chance and I will not rest until my journey is complete. We don't know how much time we have on Earth, but I am now living in the moment and making the best of it.

I love you Cade....you truly are my miracle child!

Amanda Rudd

Nathaniel, 8 Years Old

This diary was created in hopes of finding a cure for Nathaniel's disease, as well as for finding support and prayers along the way. My son, Nathaniel, was diagnosed with a horrible disease called Duchenne's Muscular Dystrophy in the Summer of 2009. As new things occur, I have been adding them to the diary. Like a blog, the beginning of the diary starts at the bottom and proceeds to the top, which has the most recent experience.

October 11, 2010

My husband has just one last duty station to attend before retiring out of the U.S. Navy. He just left this morning to San Diego, California, for two years. Of course, he'll come home every chance he can get, but it won't be the same until he is settled and back in our arms at home for good. I am full of tears this morning and I am trying to be strong, but it's hard to be away from your best friend and the best husband in the world. Nathaniel is taking it well, not a tear shed. He says he's going to help Mommy stop crying. He's such a rock when it comes to goodbyes.

August 27, 2010

Nathaniel has decided to join Cub Scouts this year. He is excited because they have a rocket camp and camping activities set up all year. He has meetings every Tuesday night. He is very happy and enjoyed the first meeting tonight where they went outside and launched rockets and played soccer ball. His uniform is in the mail and he's ready to get going on the badges!! I am happy he has found a sport/activity that he can do and not have to overexert himself.

August 23, 2010

Nathaniel started 2nd grade at a brand new elementary school this year. He is riding the bus to and from school each day and his grandmother (my husband's mother) is helping to get him on and off the bus when I'm at work. His new school teacher was not aware of Nathaniel's condition, so we had to start at ground zero again to make sure everyone at the school knew to limit outdoor, prolonged activities, walk-a-thons, etc. I made a new IEP Individual Education Plan for the new school year and we are working on a special education bus for the future. The steps are getting a little harder to use on the buses.

August 7, 2010

Nathaniel will celebrate his 8th birthday this Saturday. He wants a Super Mario party and he's been planning for months. He lights up every time he tries to come up with ideas and games for his party. Yes, some are a little far fetched. I don't think Mommy can dress as Princess Peach and Daddy dress as Bowser (the bad turtle/dragon looking guy) but we'll make the best party he can have. My dad is bringing his magic tricks to do a little show for the kids and we'll have a bounce house with a water slide inside.

July 12-16, 2010

We had a family trip to Walt Disney World in Orlando, Florida, this week! Nathaniel and I flew to Orlando from Dallas and Nathaniel vomited about 5 times before we even got on the plane on Saturday, July 10. I thought it was a fluke or just something he ate, but by Tuesday at Disney World, he started to feel worse and he had a high fever that would not go away, even through the night. I gave him Motrin and Tylenol every 5 hours to keep it down. Then his fever shot up to 104, so we took him into the emergency room at 4 a.m. and they said he had a middle ear infection and laryngitis. We got antibiotics and that night, even with the antibiotics and the Tylenol every 4 hours, his fever went back up to 104. He said to me, "Mommy, do you know how to pray?" and I said, "Yes, honey, I do" and he said "Can you pray for me to get better?" I teared up and said a quiet prayer. Then I woke him up to give him the Tylenol again and he said he saw a white light in his eyes. I teared up and stayed up the rest of the night to get the fever down. By day 3, the antibiotics started working and he was well enough to go back to Disney World. He was weak the whole time we where there. We had to roll him in a wheelchair so he wouldn't get so tired from all the walking involved at Disney World. All in all, he was so happy and loved Disney World and I was the happiest mommy ever to get a whole week off of work to spend with my son and my family.

May 17, 2010

Nathaniel is still doing great and has not had strep, flu or pneumonia in over a year! I have figured out why, too. When he was diagnosed, I asked God to take illnesses away from him and give them to me. Sure enough I've been getting the flu, strep and all sorts of things that my son used to get instead of me. I am grateful for him not having to get sick anymore. My body is healthy enough to recuperate; my son has a weakened immune system due to taking the steroids. He is still taking Prednisone and Prevacid daily. He is still happy and enjoying life. He is ready for summer to begin.

March 13, 2010

Nathaniel wants to sign up for soccer and keeps asking me when soccer starts this year. I don't have the heart to tell him he can't do any straining sports. From here on out, anything strenuous on his muscles can expedite the muscle deterioration and that's the last thing he needs. It breaks my heart that he can't play anymore, so we are going to try and sign him up for something less straining on the muscles.

February 25, 2010

Blog for Nathaniel's book. Well, after not getting sick for a whole year, Nathaniel came into my room at 4 a.m. this morning saying that he was feeling unbalanced and that his lips were dry. So I jumped up quickly, turned on the lights and saw that he was beat red in his face, especially. I checked his temperature and it was high. His fever has come and gone all day, between doses of Tylenol to keep it down. The highest point was 102 this afternoon. His Doctor checked for strep and checked his ears- nothing, thank god. We're back home now. We think he's got the stomach virus that has been spreading through neighbors and myself, because he started vomiting when he got home. I pray it was just a stomach bug and no more. Either way, he's not feeling well but excited that grandma is coming to watch him. He gets another day of no school and his most favorite part is that he gets to play Wii and Xbox. Ahhh, the life of a child. Don't you love it?

February 17, 2010

Nathaniel lost his first tooth today! I've decided I'll be writing a book about this whole experience, perhaps journal style with photos. Not sure what the name will be. Ideas and suggestions for what type of book I should write are welcome. It'll be several years down the road, but I'm documenting all my thoughts as they happen each month here on this blog.

February 16, 2010

The heart EKG went well today. The doctor told Nathaniel that he has a strong heart like Spiderman and he won't need a check up for 2 years!!!!!! Thank you, God!!!!!!!!!!!!!!!!!!!!!!!!!!

January 18, 2010

Learning about stretching exercises for my son today and put a detailed medical record together so I can quickly access his doctor's info, prescriptions and shot records.

January 14, 2010

Here's the update on Nathaniel after the appointment with the Specialists at Children's Medical Center in Dallas today. His appointment was 3 hours long, consisting of a lung test, a heart test (Doctor said his heart is abnormal) not sure what that quite means, but they are scheduling a EKG on his heart and an appointment to test lung function too, height, weight, blood pressure (a little high), a dietician came in and spoke about his diet and what foods he should be eating while on Prednisone (she suggested lower the salt intake), Physical Therapist (suggested stretch therapy on his legs daily- I do this already at night..but she gave us a DVD of exactly how to do the stretches), Occupational Therapist (she wrote up a memo to give to his school regarding things he should be doing in school- i.e. be allowed to rest when he gets tired, be allowed to leave the classroom early to beat the crowds, etc.), a Physician's Assistant who explained the side effects of the steroids and explained the vomiting is a side effect of the steroid and suggested a prescription for a dissolvable Nexium to take every day, and the Doctor came in and explained that Nathaniel has a duplication type of Duchennes Muscular Dystrophy and said that only 6% of children diagnosed with DMD have this type. She said there is not any trials or studies on duplication type DMD. We asked about some of the trials we've read on, but she said they aren't for duplications. She suggested keeping him on the same low dose of Prelone (1/2 tsp) and gave us prescriptions for Nexium. We are so happy that so many specialists could see him in one day. It's like God's hands were a part of all of these Doctors there. We felt so relieved after leaving the office today. The good part is, they said his legs are still strong and show no signs of weakness yet.

June 2009

Where to start, it's been a rough past couple of years between my son getting sick constantly and my husband going to Iraq for a year..and now this diagnosis.

I'm a mother to my 6-year-old son, who was recently diagnosed with Muscular Dystrophy. On July 10, he'll have blood work drawn to see which type it is exactly, DMD or BMD. My husband and I are just heartbroken and full of tears. It's still difficult to hold back tears. He is our only child; his name is Nathaniel. He is such a sweet and loving boy. He hugs me quite often and kisses me on the cheek every single day, even if I don't ask for a kiss. Even if I'm asleep, he'll come and give me a kiss good morning or good night on my cheek. He is a cuddle child and I love every minute of it! He says, " I love you," all the time and blows kisses and gives me tons of hugs before getting on his school bus every morning.

It is hard to leave and go to work, knowing I'll miss him coming home from school. It breaks my heart to be in a financial situation that I have to continue working, knowing this diagnosis. It is very difficult for me to not spend every minute with him, even more so now that it's summer time and he is out of school. I have a great federal job, but family is more important. If it means spending more time with my son, I'll even work nights. It doesn't matter. He's my life and he is what matters. I'll let you know how that progresses. I am still trying to figure that out. Right now need that stability as my husband will retire from the military in 2 years. But meanwhile, we are spending every minute with our child, just enjoying him and living in the moment.

Sharon Gonzolas

Benjamin, 6 Years Old

and he rides...

It has been one year since we found out that our precious son has Duchenne Muscular Dystrophy. A lifetime has passed since that November day, though in some ways, it seems like yesterday.

We always knew that Benjamin, our son, was a little slower than others his age. He, being the youngest of our six children, was constantly carried and babied. When he was born, we were overjoyed that the Lord gave us another son.

Whenever we had a well-check visit at the pediatrician, we would ask the doctor about Benjamin not meeting certain milestones. We were always told that he would catch up and that he was just held and babied too much. Our doctor was very laid back (which we liked). Finally, when Benjamin was 21 months old and not walking yet, I stood firm wanting to know if there was something wrong. Our doctor referred us to an orthopedic specialist and we set up an appointment. He took his first steps a few days before the appointment, but we went anyway.

At the time of our appointment, our daughters were 11, 9, and 7 and loved being little mommies. Our other sons were 5 and 3. The doctor took x-rays of Ben's hips and performed some other physical tests. His official diagnosis was that my daughters carried him around too much and he was just lazy. I knew that this was true. They *did* carry him around all the time. From that day forward, we decided that he needed to walk and we weren't going to carry him all the time.

Over the next few years, we lived a busy life of homeschooling, of being a pastor's family, and of sports and music activities. We never really gave too much thought to Benjamin's "slowness." We figured it was what it was and he would eventually catch up. I would continue to ask about certain things at his yearly check up, like the fact that he couldn't run or ride a bike. I was always given the same answer. He is fine. He'll catch up. He is lazy.

On Thanksgiving 2009, we were sitting around talking after dinner. Benjamin walked over to where my mom, my husband's step-mom, and I were sitting. He didn't have shoes on and my mom said something about it looking like he had flat feet. So we were talking about some of his physical delays and I mentioned that I would likely call the pediatrician to see if there was anything other than laziness going on.

On November 28, 2009, just 2 days after our conversation on Thanksgiving, we were at a birthday party. Everyone was having a good time, eating food, watching their cousin open his presents, cake, games, and visiting with family that we had not seen in a while. My husband mentioned to me that it looked like Ben's face was swelling. This had happened one other time, earlier the same year (ironically at my daughter's birthday party). When it happened the first time, we were told that if it was an allergic reaction to something and it happened again, it could be far worse. We decided it would be best if we took him to the emergency room, just to be safe. We kept debating about what to do. He didn't look as bad as the first time and wasn't having any difficulty breathing or anything like that. He seemed okay, but we thought it would be a good idea to have him looked at.

We left the birthday party to start making our way home, about an hour away. We made a stop on the way home so the children could see Hoover Dam (the Ohio version!). We decided to take him to Children's Close to Home, the urgent care for children that is close by. We got there at about 8:05 pm and they had closed at 8. Because he really seemed like he was fine, I contemplated whether or not to take him downtown to Nationwide Children's Hospital. Honestly, I hate going down there on a Saturday night. I called my husband and he said I should go ahead and go, just to make sure nothing else was going on.

We went. The doctor we saw was a resident doctor and she was very easy to talk to. She wanted to see if he had a rash anywhere, which would show if it was truly an allergic reaction or not. She lifted his shirt and didn't see anything. She proceeded to pull up his pant legs to check for a rash on his legs. I heard her say, "It looks like he has a charley horse," and then to him, "Just relax your leg." I didn't think anything of it. Then she looked at his other one and she said that it looked like he had a charley horse there, too. Normally, I wouldn't have said anything. We knew what our trusted pediatrician had said all along, that he was lazy, that he'd catch up. I firmly believe that the Lord prompted me to tell her that he has always had some trouble with walking. It felt strange to say it out loud; here he was, five years old and had trouble walking and I had done nothing about it. I really felt like I was a negligent parent at that moment.

Right after I said it, her wheels started turning and she began to ask me some other questions about his physical abilities. I suddenly realized that this wasn't about an allergic reaction anymore. She left the room and came back with a few other doctors. At this point, I didn't fully comprehend what was going on. They had Benjamin sit on the floor and watched him get up. It seemed odd. He wasn't a baby; he was five!! Why were they watching him get off the floor? What seemed normal *for him* was not normal at all. I started hearing the words "gait," "Gower's maneuver," "Yes, it looks like a waddle," all while they were talking to each other. I started feeling a bit uneasy, knowing that they saw something and there was an excitement in the room. Not a "happy" excitement, more of a, "We see something here that we don't normally see" kind of excitement.

After they watched him walk and asked me a few other questions, they said to me, "We strongly recommend that you have him seen by a neurologist." A neurologist? Isn't that a brain doctor? They explained that a neurologist looks at the entire nervous system and that they felt that he might have Muscular Dystrophy.

Muscular Dystrophy. My mind began to see images of kids with metal braces on their legs or in wheelchairs . I began to think of collecting money from my neighbors for the Jerry Lewis telethon when I was in 5th grade. What exactly *is* Muscular Dystrophy? Is it M.S? The doctor said that they called our pediatrician to get a referral, and called the neurologist and that they would be expecting my call. It seemed like it wasn't really my life. I know that sounds strange, but this sort of thing happens to other families, right? We have 6 healthy children, don't we?? Strangely, I was calm on the way home, a little confused, but calm. I called my husband and told him they that thought he had Muscular Dystrophy. I think he was as confused as I was. Didn't we take him to the E.R. because he had an allergic reaction? I told him we would talk when I got home and share everything the doctors said. My next call was to my mom. Confusion again. Where did this come from?

When I got home, I explained everything I knew to my husband, which really wasn't much. It was about midnight and he was preaching the next morning, so he went on to bed. I stayed up and googled Muscular Dystrophy. There was so much information and it was all very confusing. I had no idea that there were 9 different kinds! As I read the symptoms of them all, I was able to narrow it down. I prayed, "Please Lord, if he has to have this, please don't let it be Duchenne". Out of the nine, it was the most severe, and also the most common. As I read through the symptoms, my heart sank. He had every single symptom, except one. I just knew that our life was about to change. I was horrified to read that kids with Duchenne Muscular Dystrophy were typically in wheelchairs by the age of 10-12 and had a life expectancy of late teens. That really threw me! *My son could have a fatal disease?!* My husband let the congregation know the next morning and asked them to pray for Ben and for us as his parents to have wisdom in taking the next shaky steps. I am so thankful that the Lord has been with me through this. He is a comfort to me.

The next few weeks were a blur of doctor visits, sadness, searching for information, tears. We got in with the neurologist within 2 weeks of the E.R. visit. They did some physical tests and blood tests. We had a CK test and a DNA test. The CK test would show if there was a muscle disorder and the DNA test would show exactly what it was. We received the results of the CK test first. Normal range is less than 200 and Ben's was 17,771. Again, I knew this is what he had. We received a call that the DNA test results were in and that we should come in. On December 29, 2009, we heard the words that we already knew deep down. Our son has Duchenne Muscular Dystrophy.

Before we received the "official" diagnosis, I had already decided to make some changes. After spending weeks of sadness, crying, and depression, my husband lovingly communicated with me that being sad all the time really isn't beneficial for me, Benjamin, or the other children. As much as I still hurt from the diagnosis, I knew deep down that he was right. We needed to accept what it is and move on. It was truly freeing. I was not bound by my sadness anymore. I knew that our family would continue living life without DMD ruling it, but there would also be a new kind of normal.

There is a story in the Bible that talks about a man who was born blind. Jesus' disciples asked him why he was born blind. Did the man sin? What about his parents? Did they sin? Is this why he was blind? Jesus answered them and said that neither the man nor his parents sinned, but that the works of God would be made manifest in him. This man was healed from his blindness that very day. This passage of Scripture has been a huge comfort to me. (John 9:1-25)

Don't get me wrong. There is still a sadness, knowing what is to come. I am not bound by it now. I have learned that taking it one day at a time is best for our family. When we received the official news, they told us that the ages of 6-7 are the "honeymoon" years. He was 5, almost 6. They told us to live it up and enjoy life now. So I did.

We started steroids in January, along with a lot of vitamins and supplements. I started a facebook page, called Duchenne Muscular Dystrophy MOMS, with the intention of meeting some other moms going through the same thing. I had no idea it would turn into something so much more. The wonderful moms in the DMD community are so willing to share their stories, advice, and encouragement. I am forever grateful.

In March, about 2 months after starteding the steroids, my son rode a tricycle for the first time in his life. He can run now, too. I know that there are folks who don't agree with steroids, and honestly, it is for each family to decide what is best for them. I am glad that we chose this route. I feel it has given him some time to be a little boy, to do little boy things, like running and playing, riding his bike, and the energy to keep up with his siblings and friends.

We have had so much fun in the last year, enjoying life, visiting friends, doing things that we kept putting off. We are enjoying it now. In the back of my mind, it is always there. We home school, so I get to spend lots of time with my children when they are at their best. We are involved in our church, music lessons, and other activities. We now have incorporated clinic visits, physical therapy appointments, and occupational therapy into our schedule. *The new normal.* Our story is still being written and I want to enjoy the ride as much as I can with the family that the Lord has blessed me with.

Laura LaPat

Nicholas, 4 (Dads)

How do you write a letter to your son knowing that you may live longer than he does? How do you explain it to your family, friends, or even harder, to yourself? I do not know much about DMD, except for what the doctors have explained to me and, of course, what I have found on the Internet. What I do know is that it's not good, not good at all. So as I sit here on this nice, sunny day in December with all these feelings running through my mind to pen then to paper, I will try to hold myself together as I write this letter to my son.

To my son, Nicholas,

When you came into my life, I knew I was meant to be your father. When you first looked into my eyes with those big brown eyes, I melted and we had an instant bond. I would sit up late at night and just watch you sleep. You were so innocent and ready to take on the would. You were my perfect Miracle.

As time went on and you turned 1, you were a big ball of joy. Always smiling, and giggling everyday. You would sing bedtime songs and ride your red rocket around the house. I was always trying to get off work early so we had time to play before bed. I would watch your mom rock you to sleep and I thank god for the gifts of love I have received.

When you turned 2, you would run and talk all the time. We would do everything together. I took you to your first Giants' baseball game. You were great the whole time as I tried to explain all the situations in the game. I often would think to myself, would you be a linebacker? Or maybe a second baseman like me? How fun it was going to be for me to coach your baseball or soccer team.

Then when you turned 3, our life would change forever. You would spend the first part of 2010 in and out of the hospital. I did not know what to do. Then the doctors said the word, "Duchenne!" My heart hit the floor. All my dreams I had for you went out the window. I thought to myself, these were not your dreams, but my dreams. I am here to watch you live your life and your dreams to the fullest. It is no longer about my "sports dreams" for you, but just about you.

It was time for you to start preschool with the school district. We had a few meeting with them trying to explain your situation. They assured us they would meet all your needs, which made us happy . They also said you would be getting picked up and dropped off everyday by the little, yellow school bus. So that next Tuesday ,we explained to you that the bus was coming to pick you up. You seemed a little hesitant. Once that bus turned the corner and you saw it coming, your face lit up with the biggest smile. You said, "Mommy, is that bus for me?" Mommy said yes and you said, "I love it." That's when I knew everything would work out.

So as you turn 4 this December 22, 2010, I sit here and watch you play with your big smile, huge heart and your joyful laugh . I know everything will work out as God intended . We will together live our lives to the fullest and make all your dreams come true.

There is not a day that goes by that I don't think about that word, "Duchenne," and what it is doing to you. But it's just a word, not who you are. We can overcome it together. If we don't succeed in your lifetime, I will fight on in your honor to help find a cure. You are and always will be my Little Miracle and I will love you forever.

Love, your Dad, Sal

Carter, 7 Years Old

Only three days in, we discovered just how difficult and rewarding this parenting thing can be. It was the one of the hardest and happiest days of my life. My son, Carter Blaze, was born on February 2, 2004, at 3:36 pm. He was 5 pounds, 11 ounces, and 18.5 inches long. He was absolutely gorgeous, so alert with huge brown eyes and he immediately stole our hearts. We were so happy to have a beautiful baby boy and he appeared to be in perfect health. That appearance began to change pretty quickly; Carter refused to eat. The next day, even though he still hadn't eaten, he began to spit up. It was a light yellowish color. The pediatrician wasn't worried at first. He said Carter just needed some time to have his first bowel movement and then all would be well. He said we could go home as soon as he pooped. That afternoon the spit up started turning green and his belly swelled into the evening. He was confined to the nursery for observation. I sat up with him most of the night. I woke up at 6 o'clock and went straight to the nursery to check on Carter. The pediatrician was in with him and came right out to speak with me. The first thing he asked was if anyone in my family had cystic fibrosis. My heart sank.

The doctor began to explain that a transport team from Loma Linda University Children's Hospital was on its way to pick Carter up and take him by ambulance to the NICU where they could do further testing. They believed Carter had something called meconium ileus, an intestinal blockage that occurs frequently in newborns with cystic fibrosis. The transfer team got there and worked immediately to stabilize him. He arrived at the NICU dehydrated with a blood sugar of 240. Still very calm and alert, he was an "old soul" from the start. Several tests were run that day and confirmed there was an obstruction in his small intestine. He was scheduled for exploratory surgery the next morning. Although we had no family history of cystic fibrosis, they took several vials of blood to send for genetic cystic fibrosis screening. They didn't want to waste any time getting an official diagnosis if surgery showed meconium ileus.

On Thursday, February 5th, we got to the hospital before the sun was up and sat and rocked Carter while we waited for his turn in the operating room. We took a ton of pictures and focused on snuggling and enjoying our gorgeous newborn son who was about to have major surgery. We knew it was serious, but that didn't overshadow the happiness. At that moment, nothing in the world mattered but being able to hold that sweet baby. I could have rocked him for days.

The overwhelming fear didn't hit me until it was Carter's turn to go downstairs. His nurse brought him out to the elevator and gave our family members in the waiting room a chance for a quick hello. Then my husband, Chris, and I got in the elevator and rode down to the operating room with Carter and his nurse. The doors opened into a small area with a big set of double doors leading to the operating rooms. We had just a minute to kiss him and say our goodbyes and he was off to surgery. The two of us rode back in the elevator alone. That elevator ride was terrible. It was the first time I even considered the thought that it might not all be okay. I realized just how close we could be to total disaster and could think of nothing but holding that sweet boy again. All of the emotion from the past few days hit me at once. Carter was going to be okay; he just HAD to be okay!

His surgery started off laparoscopic and was supposed to last a little over an hour. Close to 3 hours later, his surgeon stepped off the elevator. We got the best news imaginable. Everything went well. Carter was going to be just fine! He didn't have meconium ileus. He had what's called a type 1 ileal atresia (his small intestine was closed off just before it attaches to the colon). It meant a more complicated surgery; Carter lost 12cms of his small intestine. But, it also meant there was no reason to think he had cystic fibrosis! The Dr. said he would grow up to be healthy and shouldn't have any long term problems. He said that if all went according to plan, Carter could be home in 5 days. We were overjoyed. Ecstatic. I learned what "happy tears" really are and again began to look forward to a long future with my son. I will never forget that amazing moment. Before we became parents, I don't think any of us understand just how intense the emotions that come along with it are. It is immense love that I think I only truly realized when faced with the possibility of losing it all. You begin to see the big picture and quickly recognize what is important in life and what is not.

Carter ended up with an infection after surgery and had a bumpier NICU ride than we hoped for. He was there a full month before we were able to bring him home. He was such a sweet and beautiful baby, an absolute joy. We hadn't seen the last of his health problems, though. Throughout his early years, Carter was diagnosed with reflux, asthma, anaphylactic food allergies, short bowel syndrome and growth hormone deficiency. He was sick frequently and had tubes placed in his ears at age two. Carter was also slightly behind in gross motor skills, but close enough to "normal" that no one worried. He started walking shortly after 15 months and didn't attempt to run until after he was two. Before growth hormone treatment, he was far below normal on the growth charts. We were told he'd catch up to his peers with milestones as he caught up in size.

Shortly after his third birthday, Carter began complaining of his back and legs hurting when he was walking and started asking to be carried when we were out. He was sick a lot during this time, often running high fevers for a few days with no other symptoms. In April, 2007, his pediatrician became concerned with his continued illnesses and pain. She decided we needed to run tests to rule out bone infection, auto immune disorders and cancer. They drew blood that day and made a follow up appointment the next week to go over the results. We were devastated at those possibilities but stayed optimistic. After what seemed like an eternity, we returned to the doctor for his results and were told everything was normal, that the fevers were viral and maybe he was faking his pain so we would carry him. We were told to not pick him up as much, to make him walk. We accepted this and moved on, thinking we had gotten incredibly lucky once again. We pushed him to walk more, to learn to pedal his tricycle and do the other physical things kids his age were doing. These things were difficult for Carter and he struggled, but we continued to push him since that's what we'd been told to do. It was a very frustrating time for us all.

In July that year, we had a six-month follow up with one of our favorite doctors, Carter's gastrointestinal specialist, and we were expecting a great report. The doctor, however, was troubled by some recent endocrinology blood work and advised us that Carter's liver enzymes were elevated. He saw Carter's large calf muscles and asked him to sit down on the floor and then stand. He watched as Carter used his hands to help himself up and ordered more blood work to find the cause of the elevated enzymes. One of those tests was for a creatine kinase (CK) level. That appointment was on Friday afternoon; I received a call the first thing Monday morning and was asked to bring Carter in immediately for repeat blood work. I was also informed that we had an appointment the next day with a pediatric neurologist. The nurse couldn't tell me what the appointment was for, but promised the doctor would explain it all the next day. When I took him in for the blood test that afternoon, I glanced at the new order and saw it was for a CK level. As much as I knew I shouldn't, I went home and started googlin.

I found that a high CK level along with elevated liver enzymes points towards a muscular problem. When I added my son's age into my searches, I started seeing the words Duchenne Muscular Dystrophy. I was shocked to find out that not only is 1 in 3,500 boys born with Duchenne, they are left unable to walk by their teens and it's rare for them to live into their 30's! It is a progressive muscle-wasting disease with no cure; most young men die as a result of heart and lung failure in their teens or early 20's. How had I not heard of this before?!?! As I kept reading, I realized Carter had many of the symptoms. He didn't walk until 15 months, was delayed in speech, and although he couldn't ride a tricycle and complained of muscle aches, his body was well defined and appeared muscular all over. My heart crumbled. It was clear why we were so urgently being sent to yet another specialist. We'd had many health scares in the past; I didn't want to accept this. But, in my heart, I just knew. My mind was suddenly thrown back into that intense fear of losing my baby. I again vowed that he was going to be okay; he HAD to be okay.

Carter's first appointment with neurology confirmed my nightmare. It was almost certain he had Duchenne Muscular Dystrophy. They drew blood at that first neurology appointment that confirmed the diagnosis. Carter's doctors don't think that his various medical conditions have anything to do with each other. Although he always had medical conditions, we weren't prepared for a truly life-changing diagnosis like this. You never can be. It's been a tough three and a half years dealing with our new reality. We are beginning to see Carter's strength and stamina decline and that brings its own set of emotions. It's painful to watch my son struggle and know there's nothing I can do to stop it. As parents we are somewhat helpless and have to trust that there will be a cure in time for our son. He has the benefit of being young in a time of great medical advancements and we will never give up hope. Carter uses a manual wheelchair for long distances and was just prescribed an electric scooter for school. These are big steps for us, but Carter seems relieved each step of the way. He's kept us strong since day one. We feel we're the luckiest parents in the world to have been trusted to raise him. He's amazing and has always had something special about him, a spark. I know that, regardless of his physical abilities, and anything he goes through medically, Carter is incredibly smart and will accomplish great things in his life. I can't wait to be here and have a front row seat for them all.

Duchenne is a heartbreaking disease. But, it can be a blessing. It has become our daily reminder that nothing can be taken for granted, not a second of our lives. There isn't anything more important than the time we have with our loved ones. We need to slow down and connect, live each day like it is our last and realize how lucky we are to have the people we do in our lives.

Rhiannon

Joshua, 7 Years Old

When Joshua was born in 2003, the CPK test was mandatory on all boys. This is how we learned the words "Duchenne Muscular Dystrophy". We had never heard these words before. I was then tested and am not a carrier. We were told 1 in 3,500 boys is born with this disease every year. Only 6% of those are born with this disease by 'fluke,' and 2% of those have duplications, which Joshua has. While we were absorbing the new words, Duchenne Muscular Dystrophy, we were then told what to expect. We were told it is an incurable disease. The life expectancy is approximately 18 years of age. Our son would be in a wheelchair by his 8th birthday and graduate to a breathing tube and full time hospital care by the age of 16. He may never be able to ride a bike, swing on a swing set, jump, climb, or do many things a normal child does. "There is nothing we can do." Nothing we can do?

This news sent us into mourning. My son is going to die! No matter what I do, my son is going to die. Then it dawned on me. Of course my son will die. So will I! Someday, we all will--eventually. When it's his turn, it's his turn, but that doesn't mean I'm going to let this be the reason he dies, without a fight. The gloves came off and the fight for his life started.

If it weren't for the internet, Joshua wouldn't be where he is today. At age 3 the steroids started. Along with the steroids came a multitude of vitamins and supplements to counteract the side-effects. This is also when physiotherapy, occupational therapy and speech therapy started; the first pair of "bedtime boots" were made, massaging the legs became routine and our diet changed. What really changed was our life.

How many 3 year-old boys can listen to their bodies? Mine learned to. If his body needed to rest, he rested. Whatever his body needed, he did. He drank, he ate, and he learned to tell us what his body needed. This became an instinct, not a choice.

Joshua was using the Gower's Movement to raise himself from the floor, but once everything started, he didn't do it anymore. He began running, jumping, climbing, swinging, and riding a bike. First, a tricycle, then training wheels, then no training wheels, and now a bigger bike! He can do it!

Once Joshua started school, we learned he had the greatest principal we could ask for. Unfortunately, the principal's cousin was affected by this same disease and passed quite some time ago. But he knew this disease. He understood. This twist of fate was regrettably a huge benefit.

As soon as school started, Joshua was able to have physiotherapy in the classroom during circle time. He was understood because the IEP (Individual Education Plan) meetings started. We, the teachers, the resource workers, the physiotherapists and the principal were all reading the same notes, calling regarding any concerns, asking questions, and everyone was involved in every answer.

Joshua was given a "friend'" from an older grade to help him, if needed, at recess to climb things, get on the swings if they were too high, or pull him in a sleigh in the winter if his legs were tiring. His needs were adapted to because his body's needs are instincts.

For Joshua to get to school, he rides a bus. Once kindergarten was over and he was to take the bus every day instead of 2 or 3 times per week, a new bus with a lift, an extra step, and double handrails was ordered for him. He only uses the lift when his legs are sore, but it is considered his bus.

Having a son with a disease this serious, which we had never heard of, lets us grow in a different way. We learn from him. He has taught us the real meaning of empathy. He has taught us to appreciate and live each moment to its fullest. He has also taught us that life is too short, so while we are here, we need to learn, understand, and teach. We are the only ones who can fight for our children, but when there are many of us fighting for our own child together, our voices get louder.

Words I live by are: Everything happens for a reason. We may not know why right now, but life will tell us--when we're ready.

Naomi Clark-Desender

Fonte, 9 Years Old

Fonte Xiong was born on a warm summer day, June 18th, 2001. He was a healthy happy baby boy. After a full 24 hours in the hospital, Fonte and I were discharged to go home. It was one of the happiest moments in my life. I was holding my beautiful baby boy and I had my wonderful 2 year old daughter, Lysia. Life was looking great!

My husband, Yia, stayed home with me for a week before returning to work. I enjoyed spending my days with Fonte and my daughter. But that happiness was short lived. By the time Fonte was a toddler, I started noticing that he wasn't reaching the developmental milestones as were most children his age. When I took him for doctors' appointments, they said boys tend to be slower than girls and for us not to be too concerned. We waited and waited, but by 16 months, Fonte was still having difficulty walking. He was still crawling more than walking and, when he was walking, he was holding onto furniture. Still, his pediatrician did not seem concerned and so we trusted his judgment.

Fonte finally started walking by the time he was eighteen months. At that time we noticed that Fonte had extremely large calves, and my mother-in-law started calling him Popeye because of his enlarged muscles. We thought nothing of it; his doctors didn't seem too worried about it either. But I remember specifically one day at the mall. We took him out of his stroller to let him roam around, and he would walk clumsily for a little bit and then put his arms up for us to hold him. People we knew started saying we were babying him too much and we needed to let him grow. But we treated him just like we treated our daughter. We definitely weren't babying him.

By the time Fonte started school, we started to notice that he was really behind. At the early childhood screening before he started preschool, he failed every single test. It confirmed my fears at that time. I looked around and saw that most children were able to hop on one foot, or follow directions from one test to another. One of the ladies sat me down after looking through Fonte's results and asked me if I had any concerns about Fonte's milestones. I finally was able to tell her that he was developing more slowly than most children his age, at least from what I was seeing, and that his speech and motor skills were not developing normally, either. She said she was going to refer his case to the special ed department. They would come and do an assessment on Fonte to determine his developmental status. I agreed to do this.

A few weeks later they came to our house to do the assessment. At that time, they found out that Fonte has a mild learning disability, but it was not severe enough to need any intervention at the time. He finally started preschool.

He had half-day preschool. Some days when he didn't take the bus, and I dropped him off, I noticed that while all the other kids sat together, Fonte sat alone. His teacher also noticed his social skills were lacking and that he had extreme fatigue. She called me almost every single night to ask if he was getting enough sleep and would tell me about his day at school. She mentioned one specific time when they were walking across the street and he could not keep up with the other children. She said that he complained of fatigue all the time. I told her that he was getting about ten hours of sleep and that I also noticed that no matter how much sleep he got, he just wasn't as active as his cousins or neighbors.

His teacher was a kind lady who really cared about Fonte. She suggested that we take him in to see his pediatrician. I told her that he had a physical scheduled already and that we would ask his pediatrician at that time. But a few weeks later, Fonte's clinic called to say his pediatrician wouldn't be in and that we should reschedule. I knew that we couldn't wait, so I asked for another pediatrician. We were then scheduled with Dr. Warnken. Because I had just started a new job, Yia was to take Fonte in for this exam. I made sure that Yia mentioned Fonte's extreme fatigue and enlarged calf muscles.

On the day of Fonte's physical, Yia went in, pulled up Fonte's pants and showed Dr. Warnken his calves, and explained that although Fonte was sleeping ten hours a day, he was still very tired all the time. Dr. Warnken felt Fonte's calves, had him walk for him and said that he wanted to draw some blood to check for muscle disease. So Yia agreed to that and two tubes of blood were drawn in mid- November.

A week passed. One day before Thanksgiving, while at work, I receive the most devastating news of my life. I was checking my home voice mails, and there was a call from Dr. Warnken himself stating that he had the test results back and he needed us to call him back as soon as possible. I knew this was not good because the majority of the time, the doctors never call. My stomach sank to the floor. I picked up the phone at work and called him. His nurse answered and said he would call me back as soon as he was done with a patient. Fifteen minutes later, he called and said that they checked Fonte's CPK levels (Creatine phosphokinase). When a muscle is damaged, CPK leaks into the bloodstream. When the total CPK level is very high, it usually means there has been injury or stress to the heart, the brain, or muscle tissue. Determining which specific form of CPK is high helps doctors determine which tissue has been damaged. The doctor said Fonte's level was very high and that he thought Fonte might have a muscle disease called muscular dystrophy.

I had never heard of muscular dystrophy before and asked him what that meant. He simply said that it meant Fonte had muscle weakness. His CPK results were at about 27,000. A normal CPK level would be around 0-300 . I was so shocked that Fonte's were so exrememly high. The doctor wanted us to go back in immediately for more lab work. I agreed to schedule it for Monday since we had already planned to spend Thanksgiving with my parents and family out of town.

As soon as I got off the phone with Dr. Warnken, I looked up muscular dystrophy on my computer and a lot of information popped up. I pulled up the Muscular Dystrophy Association website and the information I got hit me hard. There are nine types of MD and the most common one was a condition called Duchenne Muscular Dystrophy, which affects boys only (about 99% of them are boys). When I read the symptoms of DMD, I knew immediately that this was what Fonte had. The symptoms were difficulty climbing stairs, enlarged calf muscles, inability to run or hop on one foot and, of course, fatigue. There was so much information. Towards the last few sentences, it said there was no cure and the mortality occurred at about 15-20 years old. My heart sank and immediately tears started flowing, non-stop. I called Yia at work immediately and told him about the phone call and Yia was completely quiet on the other line. We both were so scared.

On Monday, we took Fonte in for more tests to confirm the CPK levels and we also discussed with Dr. Warnken the research we had done online with MD. I told him I thought Fonte might have Duchenne Muscular Dystrophy (the most common form and the genetic childhood disease that is the number one killer) and he said he also thought the same. I asked him how he knew that Fonte might have had muscle disease when Fonte's other doctors never seemed concerned. He told me that after 30 years of being a pediatrician, he had only seen one other case with another boy whose muscles were enlarged, and so he knew the signs to look for.

On Tuesday morning, Dr. Warnken called me to confirm that Fonte definitely had some type of MD although, to be sure, he would schedule us to see Dr. Day, a neurologist specializing in neuromuscular diseases at Gillette Children's Hospital. On December 7th, 2005, we went in to meet Dr. Day. More labs were drawn to be sent to the University of Utah for genetic testing. The test would be about 99% accurate in diagnosing the muscle disease. We were to wait about 1-3 months before we would get the results back. We waited through Christmas and New Year's. Finally, on January 4th, 2006, the genetic counselor called to confirm what I had feared all along--Fonte had Duchenne Muscular Dystrophy, a progressive and fatal muscle disease. I left work immediately. I couldnt bear it anymore. And for months, Yia and I didnt see the sun shine. We couldn't even keep up with what day it was, or what time it was. The days became a blur.

We wanted to spend as much time with Fonte as possible. We wanted to make sure that every moment counted. I had just had my youngest son, Chufeng, 10 months earlier and we all wanted to make sure that we made every moment special.

By the time Fonte entered second grade, it became evident that soon, he would probably need a manual wheelchair for long distances. While waiting for insurance to approve of this, we used a stroller when possible. Fonte was very tiny for a 7-year-old and we had no problem using a baby stroller. By this time, Fonte was falling about 10-15 times a day and could no longer climb stairs. He would go down stairs on his butt and we would carry him upstairs. But despite his difficulty walking, we dreaded having to use the wheelchair and kept it in the garage the majority of the time. By the end of the shool year, it became apparent that we could no longer avoid his wheel-chair, and he started taking it to school. That summer, two weeks after Fonte's eighth birthday, my dear son lost his walking ability. Yia and I were devastated again. I didn't go to work for one whole week.

Fonte started having dreams of walking again, and he would wake up confused. His dreams seemed so real, and yet, when he woke up, he had no use of his legs. He cried a lot, and even I, as his mother, couldn't completely understand his pain. I cried in private, never wanting Fonte to see how much pain I was in and how much I feared this disease. One day, Fonte asked me if he would ever walk again, and I had to tell him the truth, that he might never walk again. I said that scientists were working really hard on trying to find a cure. Fonte was like a soilder who has lost his legs in the war but still feels his legs--except that with Fonte, he still has his legs, they just dont work. There were days when I would walk into his room and find tears in his eyes. He became a prisoner in his own body. But although he couldn't walk anymore at such a young age, he bounced back quickly.

Soon, he became his happy, old self again. A Spongebob loving kid, a selfless child who wanted to make other people happy. In every picture we took of him, he made sure he was always smiling. But there were days of deep depression, too. There were days he was so angry that he would bang his fists on the table and scream. I would just hold him. There was nothing more that I could do. I tried to calm him down and he would sob in my chest. I wanted him to know that, although I could still walk and might never truly understand, I would be with him on this journey of his. Despite any obstacles that came our way, I would be there for him. I recall one particular day, when he was seven years old. He was so tired, sitting on the stairs. He asked me what would happen if he couldn't walk again. And my reply was that when he was weak, I would try to be his strength. When he could no longer walk, I would carry him and be his legs. He was my strength, too. He made me strong and courageous. He was the most courageous person that I knew.

Today, Fonte is a brilliant, happy nine-year-old boy. He is already losing the ability to raise his arms to his mouth to feed himself. On bad days, I have to feed him. But the majority of the time, he lowers his mouth to his hands to feed himself. He is very smart and finds ways to adjust to all the changes his body is going through. Fonte has an amazing soul and is so optimistic. He has such a great outlook on life. Despite all the challenges that he has faced and will face, this precious child will persevere.

Mainhia yang

SECTION II
The Transition Phase: Fear Of The Unknown

Getting around becomes increasingly difficult, especially long distances, like at school or going shopping. The physical abilities between kids without Duchenne and the kids affected usually increases the social isolation about the time middle school rolls around. Which is when kids start wanting to fit in the most. How does a Duchenne kid who can barely climb stairs fit in, run in gym or climb the climbing wall? It soon becomes apparent, walking to the dreaded use of a wheelchair is near, normally by age twelve. This is also the phase that often brings on scoliosis of the spine, respiratory decline and maybe heart complications. Medical decisions often must be made rather quickly and can crop up almost unexpectedly. After Duchenne robs the child of walking, the arms and upper body go next. The prolonged stress and pressure of the rapid decline of the Duchenne child has the parent challenged mentally, spiritually and physically to the MAX! The little things like brushing teeth, feeding and writing become difficult. Raising hands above the head , bath-rooming, even rolling over in bed becomes impossible. The lost sports and outdoor fun dreams get buried under the realization that death is closer. It becomes imperative that one must GRAB onto the beauty of life while the child is still young. The biggest question is--how will I survive? The Duchenne parent would give anything for the madness to STOP! The fear of the unknown is suffocating. How could this horrible disease strike a child--my child?

Cam, 13 Years Old

My Special Little Soldier

You are my world.
Every time I look at you
I'm slowly dying inside.
I have to stand by and watch you
Slowly fade before my eyes.
I want so much to take it all away,
Rid you of this awful condition
And let you live the life you deserve.
So this I make my mission:
I promise I will do all I can
To give you everything you want,
To be there for you,
Every step of the way.
Through hard times and happy times,
Through joy and through pain,
Remember I will be there,
Come sunshine or come rain.
As things get harder,

I see you get stronger.
Your determination dumfounds me
And I admire you so much.
Your smile lights up your whole face
And melts my heart without a trace.
Everything is becoming a struggle,
The walking and the stairs.
Sometimes it upsets you
But remember I'll always be there.
Every second of every day I pray
They find that cure soon,
And I guarantee the day they do,
I'll jump as high as the moon
Because to be able to watch you grow
Into a very fine young man
Is something I can only dream of
And hope someday you can.
It's getting harder and harder
To hide it all from you.
You are so bright and smart and clever.
I dread the day you ask me
The hardest question of all time.
But I will be there
And will never let you down.
On me you can depend
With a smile and never a frown.
I will smile and brighten your day,
Even though I'm dark inside.
I will hold your hand
And be your strength
Whenever you are weak.
You have been through so much

And are so very brave,
The drug trials and tests,
Hospital appointments and checks.
And each time you just smile,
Occasionally get upset.
Cam you astound me
More and more each day.
I am soooo proud to be your mummy
And we will fight this all the way

Postscript

When Cam, now 11, was first diagnosed at 3 ½, our lives were turned upside down and changed forever. As a family, we set about fund-raising and giving Cam all we could, including (after much fund-raising) a dream-come-true trip to Australia for 6 weeks. He's Australia mad and couldn't wait to go, and also visit Australia zoo. Anyone who knows Cam knows what an artist he is, and also a wonderful, kind, considerate, and smiley child, in spite of everything he's going through. Over the years I have had so much I wanted to say to Cam, but never could, as, at this stage, he is still blissfully unaware of the full struggle which lies ahead for him, and he copes now as best he can with all he has to deal with. With this in mind, I finally sat down one night, tears flowing, and just wrote and wrote, one of the hardest but also easiest things I have ever had to write, straight from the heart. That is where "My Special Little Soldier" was born. It's now tucked away, and when Cam finally understands what this devastating condition means to him, Cam will finally get to read this poem and know just how much he means to us and that we'll be there always and will never give up the fight against this awful condition.

We love you always Special Soldier

Lisa Edmonds

Alex, 11 Years Old

"A son is the happy memories of the past, the joyful moments of the present, and the hope and promise of the future".

Alex, age 11, was diagnosed with Duchenne Muscular Dystrophy in November, 2004. He was 5 years old and our only child at that time. We were devastated when we learned the news, but over time we knew we would give him the best life and best care possible. We eventually found a new normal. We networked, researched and educated ourselves as we were beginning this new journey. In September 2006, we were also blessed with the birth of our twins (a boy and a girl), who are not affected by DMD.

Today, Alex is a 5th grade student and is doing very well. He is still walking, running and is a typical 11-year-old in many ways. Alex rides a motorized mobility scooter at school and for long distance trips. He is very creative and loves to build with Legos. He is a Cub Scout, about to transition to a Boy Scout. Alex also loves playing with his twin brother and sister.

Having a child with a life-threatening disease has made me learn to cherish the little things and to not take things for granted. Watching him run and play with his brother and sister or the three of them rolling around on the floor playing can bring tears to my eyes. Every time I see a child ride a bike or a skateboard down our street, my heart breaks a little. If only I could have one day or one hour of watching Alex ride a bike or skateboard. This simple childhood activity is something I will never see him do!

We pray every for a CURE!

Kim Maddux

Hawken, 13 Years Old

If You Want to Make God Laugh…I lived my life by goals and achievements, never doubting that I was in control of my destiny. My career was exciting; the income was incredible. I traveled and shopped wherever I wanted. I was having such a great time that I almost forgot to get married. But having one child was part of my plan, so just before my biological clock stopped ticking, I found the ultimate man…tall, handsome, smart and nice.

Given my age at marriage, and being told it could take quite a while, Paul and I decided to waste no time in getting pregnant. Paul had introduced me to Bible study while we were dating, and it became a bond between us. I was raised in a religious environment, but fell away from it as a teenager. The scripture-based study made so much more sense to me than the organized religious teaching I had learned as a child. So, it was very natural for me to pray that we would have a child soon.

Six weeks after our wedding, I was pregnant, all according to plan. Less than a year after our wedding, we had a beautiful home and a precious baby boy, Hawken. Life was good; I loved my husband and idolized my son. We did try to have another child but stopped short of IVF and decided to be grateful for our one perfect child.

Five and a half years later Hawken was going to kindergarten. For the first time since he was born, I was going to have time for myself. What would I do? I was always a horse fanatic, would I take up riding again, play golf, go back to work? Again, I prayed about it. The first thing I signed up for was an intensive seven year Bible study course. I continued to pray and study. I came across a concept that really perplexed and confused me. It had to do with, "to die to oneself." This concept did not agree with my philosophy of setting and achieving personal goals. At the same time I was dealing with this repudiation of my lifestyle, Paul and I were noticing that things weren't quite right with Hawken.

Actually, we had talked to Hawken's pediatrician several times over the previous two years about his lack of stamina. She said he was just a big kid (he was 11 pounds, 5 ounces when he was born) and that he would grow into his size. Being the mom that I am, I took him to the park to run wind sprints, thinking that he was just being lazy.

We even heard that large calf muscles and muscle weakness could be a symptom of muscular dystrophy. His pediatrician said the only way to find out was to perform a muscle biopsy, and there wasn't a weak muscle in his body to test. He went through a two hour physical and occupational therapy evaluation. We even asked them about the possibility of muscular dystrophy. A couple of weeks later, we received an eight page report that never mentioned muscular dystrophy but recommended strength training. We should have been relieved, but by then awareness was settling into our consciousness, and we started our own education. We learned that a simple blood test could diagnosis muscular dystrophy. Our pediatrician thought it was a waste of time, but agreed. That was on a Thursday afternoon, and we were promised results by Friday afternoon. At midnight on Friday, after no word from the doctor, we were up all night researching his symptoms. We learned that Duchenne was a progressive and fatal muscle wasting disease, and that there was no cure.

When the phone rang Saturday morning, we were prepared for the worst. Unless you lose a child, or have a child with a terminal illness, there is no way to describe the terror you feel when you are told that your child will live a short and very crippled life. Paul was playing with Hawken in the swing set when I called him up. He didn't need to be told the news.

Hawken was the same happy child that he was a few minutes before, the day before, all his life. Duchenne had been a part of him since conception; he hadn't changed, but the news rocked our world. I had never before experienced pain that dropped me to my knees.

"Die to oneself" became a crystal clear concept. Our life would not be as we planned, and yet, everything in our life had prepared us for this future. Paul and I are both fairly competent people. If we felt that becoming victims and living through our emotions would have been good for Hawken, we would have done that well. But we knew that it was our thinking (and praying) that would help our son, and not our emotions.

For the first time, I had absolutely no control of my life or the life of my son. There was only one place to turn, and that was to God. My closet became the place where I went to cry and to pray. One day, a couple of weeks after diagnosis, while I was praying, I received the strongest inspiration that I have ever known. That inaudible voice told me to get up and be comforted. I keep trying to re-write the message to say that Hawken would be healed and all would be fine, but that's not what I heard/felt. Since that day, I've had many moments of pain and anxiety, but I do know that we will get through this, and that there is a very definite purpose for our lives.

Hawken is now almost fourteen years old, and by Duchenne standards, he's doing very well. Probably we will never know if it's his genetic makeup or something we've done to keep him mobile and active this long. If I had to name one thing that benefited him, it would be discipline, both for Hawken and for us as his parents. Missing a day of stretching is not an option, grilled fish and chicken and steamed veggies are his basic diet. Sticking to his medication in spite of side effects and monitoring his activity as much as possible have been very important.

Along the way, we've encountered both the expected and the unexpected hurts. When we could talk about his diagnosis without falling apart, we gathered our closest friends together, knowing that they would be a strong support system for us. After the initial diagnosis, the biggest shock we got was to see those friends that we spent so much time with, fade away. One very painful day was explaining to our six-year-old son why his best friend no longer wanted to play with him. How do you explain to a six- year-old that his friend still likes him, but that he has become an inconvenience to the parents? Out of this initial group of "close" friends, only two have remained close friends and big supporters of ours.

The social isolation that comes with this disease is heartbreaking. Boys run. Boys play hard; they are competitive. Thanks to video games, Hawken can actually compete, but he misses out on sports, and he would have been such a great athlete without Duchenne; his balance and eye/hand coordination is superb.

As our old friends faded away, we have been blessed by new friends that have come into our lives with the full knowledge of our life with Duchenne. Without exception, we can connect the kids that are patient and compassionate directly to parents that have a heart of philanthropy and are insistent on instilling compassion in their kids. It's still not easy, but these families are God-sent and we love them.

Summers are especially tough. Kids are in sports camps, the beach is not an easy outing and boys are hanging out with their friends doing what boys do in summer--sports. It takes a lot of creativity and time to organize activities. And as a working mom, I'm not satisfied that I do everything possible to enrich Hawken's life. I'm looking forward to high school next year with a fresh start and a hope that kids are a bit more specialized in their interests in high school and that Hawken can meet new friends with interests in technology and video production. But each year means fewer things that Hawken can do as his strength slips away.

I've been told that I'm in denial about Hawken's future since he's still mobile. That's very possibly true, and I'm fine with that. Recently, I experienced a really big moment of denial, and it was a wonderful few minutes. Earlier this year Hawken, Paul and I got certified for scuba diving. It was a struggle for Hawken, but he was determined and he passed all of his tests. Recently, we were on a scuba vacation in the Cayman Islands. Hawken was doing well; I was having a bit of difficulty with my buoyancy. When it was time to go up, Hawken was already at the rope waiting for me to catch up. As I came close to him, he reached out to help me and pulled me in just like any big healthy teenager would help his struggling mom. It was a moment of knowing what it would be like to have a healthy son and the transfer of strength from one generation to the next. I will always cherish that moment. Fortunately, Paul just happened to capture those few seconds on the video camera. I suppose living under water or on the moon could solve many of our strength issues with Duchenne.

After one year from diagnosis, Paul and I started CureDuchenne. Our mission was three fold; we were surprised that there was no national organization with the name Duchenne in its title, and we weren't satisfied that doing things " the way they have always been done" was the route we wanted to take, since that path had not resulted in viable treatments. Since we both come from sales and marketing backgrounds, we knew that ignorance was our enemy, and that money was needed for research, but people wouldn't contribute to a disease they'd never heard of. Creating public awareness for Duchenne was a primary goal. Secondly, we wanted to establish an organization that applied business practices to research that would push the science from the labs into for-profit companies that had the resources to develop these ideas into drugs. Lastly, we wanted to share our faith with those who were interested.

CureDuchenne is by no means a religious organization. Our family is Christian, but we love, embrace and work closely with friends and families of all different faiths. We believe that there is a bigger purpose to our lives. That, and knowing that we have eternity to look forward to, have been a great source of comfort to our family. Every night, we pray together as a family. With all the opportunity that I have for feeling inadequate as a mother in this helpless situation, I am confident that we are giving Hawken the greatest gift we can give him, a relationship with God. I've been able to witness that his faith enables him to see the needs and issues of other people instead of focusing on his disease.

Many wonderful parents of Duchenne boys and young men have joined CureDuchenne in our quest for a cure. We have organized CureDuchenne to include everyone who wants to help be part of the solution. Our motto is, "Action as Therapy." Parents who are actively involved seem to be much happier and cope better. We certainly don't offer promises, and we want to make sure that families keep their faith focused on God and not on us. If there are treatments that come from our efforts, Paul and I definitely don't want standing ovations. The glory should go to God and not to us or CureDuchenne. As easy as it is to think that the ends justify the means when your child has a terminal illness, we believe that we can still operate in integrity in searching for a cure and caring for our sons.

Just this weekend, a public service announcement sponsored by Cadillac for CureDuchenne aired on NFL Football on FOX Sports. We believe that we are turning a corner for Duchenne. We don't know that a cure will come in time for Hawken, but we do know a cure will come. Duchenne has always been around, and it will always be with us. Spontaneous mutations occur where there is no family history of Duchenne, so there in no way to genetically consul the end of this disease. Since we can't eliminate it, we must cure Duchenne.

Hawken's grandfather is a polio survivor. He's probably not as tall as he might have been without being afflicted by the disease when he was younger. Our dream is that someday Hawken will explain to his grandchildren that he would have grown much taller had he not taken the steroids, which were the only drugs available for Duchenne patients before he was given the more curative therapies that saved his life. We see diabetes patients live fairly normal lives; in fact there are many examples of incurable diseases being turned into lifelong chronic conditions. Watching Magic Johnson on a sports program reminded me of how quickly a fatal disease like AIDS can be at least partially conquered with enough public awareness and action.

In Hawken's kindergarten class, the kids were asked what they wanted to be when they grew up. Hawken proudly said, "I just want to be a dad." I was in the classroom that day and had to leave the room and run to the bathroom to cry. I want more than anything to be a grandmother. To see Hawken holding his child would be a miracle--and I'm not giving up on that.

Several years ago, I had heard the cliché, "If you want to make God laugh, tell Him your plans." At the time, that didn't have a lot of meaning for me. Now, I can see that God had different plans for our lives, and we are completely out of control. All we can do now is hold on for the ride and continue to look for guidance from up above.

Debra Miller

Ryan, 10 Years Old

My son........Ryan
Beautiful Blue Eyes
Smile that makes me melt
Wicked sense of humour
Laugh that lights up a room
Enough Love in his heart to fill the ocean
My son............Ryan
Duchenne Muscular Dystrophy.........Heartbreaking

~Jane Williams

Bradley, 13 Years Old

Our lives were blessed with the arrival of our second child in March of 1997. At birth, Bradley was a healthy baby boy. His first year seemed normal and he reached developmental milestones at appropriate ages.

However, looking back on his early years, I saw things after the diagnosis that I had not realized before. I remembered that he was a cautious and slow walker while other one-year-olds walked quickly, practically running. Bradley also had difficulty walking uphill, while his peers could run up the same hill without hesitation. We thought that, with confidence, he would get faster and more proficient at walking and running.

After Bradley turned 2, we noticed he was clumsy and fell more frequently than others his age. I thought this was related to his frequent ear infections, which may have affected his balance. But after Bradley's third birthday, we realized he was not getting better. He seemed to be stumbling and falling more often. His gait, while running, seemed awkward and waddled. Others began to comment about the possibility that something was wrong. We became concerned enough to seek medical advice. Bradley's pre-kindergarten physical was scheduled in August of 2000. At this visit, I voiced my concerns but the doctor reassured me that he would grow out of this awkward stage. I was unable to accept this reassurance. I knew something was wrong.

I decided to take him to a chiropractor who told me his spine was out of alignment. He wanted to do spinal adjustments but my husband and I were uncomfortable about chiropractic treatment.

We decided to get a second opinion from a reputable pediatrician. At the time, she did not see any significant problem. She told me she would follow up with him in 6 months and refer him to physical therapy if I was still concerned. I did not want to wait 6 months but I also felt like an overly worried mother who was making a big deal over nothing. I was ready to give up.

My husband said we could not stop there. He knew a doctor personally and asked him to check on Bradley. He took x-rays in his office. He told me the x-rays were normal but he could see the waddled gait. He pondered on whether to send him to an orthopedic doctor or to a physical therapist. He decided to send him to physical therapy for gait training. On the first visit, the physical therapist told me Bradley had muscle weakness. The thought of muscular dystrophy did not enter my mind. I just felt positive that she was going to work with him and strengthen his muscles.

When I mentioned the muscle weakness to the chiropractor, he told me he had noticed his large calves and wondered if he might have muscular dystrophy. I didn't think it was possible since we had no family history of muscular dystrophy. But later that afternoon, I got my nursing books out and read about muscular dystrophy. A picture of a boy using the Gower maneuver--getting on all fours and pushing up with a hand resting on one knee to stand--reminded me of that day in class when muscular dystrophy was discussed briefly. I remembered thinking about how I had noticed Bradley getting up in the same way, but at the time dismissed it from my thoughts.

That weekend, after the physical therapy visit, I was at my parents' house. We didn't have the internet at home, so while there, I searched the internet for information on muscular dystrophy. When I read about Duchenne Muscular Dystrophy (DMD), I felt as if I was reading about my son. He had all of the symptoms; difficulty climbing stairs, a waddled gait, frequent falls, and difficulty rising from sitting. I had a very strong feeling that this was his diagnosis. I wanted to be wrong.

Bradley was referred to the neuromuscular clinic at St. Louis Children's Hospital and was seen six weeks later. It was November 14, 2000, a day we would never forget, a day that would change the rest of our lives.

Bradley was evaluated by a neurologist. As we left that day, he gave us an order for a CPK blood test and sent us to the hospital lab. He told us he would call us within the next week but we received a call one hour after getting home from St. Louis. His CPK level was 14,000, an indication that he did have muscular dystrophy. He told me he suspected Duchenne Muscular Dystrophy. We were devastated by the news.

The next step was having a gene test to confirm the diagnosis. We had to wait 4 weeks, only to find out the results of the gene test were inconclusive. I hoped the diagnosis was a mistake but the neurologist was still almost certain that he did have DMD. He told me that Bradley would need a muscle biopsy to confirm the diagnosis.

When I received the muscle biopsy results, I thought I was prepared for the worst. But when it was confirmed that Bradley had DMD, it was like getting the diagnosis all over again. I broke down and cried as the neurologist tried to comfort me. He spent more than 30 minutes talking to me on the phone that evening. Shortly after the phone call, my husband came home. I met him at the door and burst into tears as I explained to him that Bradley really did have DMD.

The night we received the initial diagnosis, I could not sleep. I tried to pray but could not find the words. I had never experienced such silence with God. I knew he was there but I thought, "Why God? What have I done to cause this? Why does my little boy have to suffer? Why can't it be me?" I then felt as if God was holding me in his arms. I do not think he expected me to know what to pray. He understood my devastation and comforted me. I was experiencing the process of grief-denial, anger, depression and guilt. In time, I realized that God had chosen my husband, Tom, and me to be Bradley's parents. God did not deliberately cause Bradley's disease, nor had this happened because I was a bad person. I knew that God had a purpose for Bradley's life and a purpose for making me and Tom part of it. I knew that God was in control and would get us through the hardships ahead.

I saw a friend in a local store and told her about Bradley's diagnosis. I began to cry in front of my two children. I could not hold back the tears. After she left, my little girl, Stephanie said, "Mommy, I think I hurt Bradley's legs." She thought she had been playing too rough with Bradley and had caused him to have muscular dystrophy. I could not believe she was blaming herself. I reassured her that it was not her fault. It was then that Bradley looked at me with a confused expression and said, "Mommy, are you crying about me?" I realized how much he knew. I recognized how open I needed to be with my children about Bradley's disease. I wanted them both to be educated about the disease on a level that they could handle and understand. On the way home from the store, I explained to Stephanie that Bradley had been born with muscular dystrophy and there was nothing she could have done to cause it.

It has been ten years since Bradley's diagnosis. For the most part, I have tried to be positive through the years. I try to think of the good things that have come out of Duchenne Muscular Dystrophy. I think of the people I have met, all the things that I have learned, and how I have come to understand others with

disabilities. I am thankful that things have not happened exactly as the neurologist predicted. We were told Bradley would be completely dependent on a wheelchair by the age of 12 years. He is going on 13 years old and continues to walk. He only uses his wheelchair occasionally for activities that require long distances.

I am thankful to all the people who have prayed for Bradley because I know God has taken care of him. I know that God will continue to take care of Bradley and carry us all through the difficulties ahead. Even if Bradley does stop walking, it will not be the end of the world. I have faith that he will lead a productive, quality life as many with disabilities have already done.

Lisa Jones

Bradley
My Brother's Diagnoses

I go about my life wondering if anyone knows what it is like to have a brother or sister with an illness or disability. I wonder if they feel the same things I do: anger, sadness, and grief. I cannot decide which pain is greater. Is it the person with the illness or the person who has to watch them go through it? As the years go by, I am learning that both are the same amount of pain. At the young age of seven, that question never went through my mind, even though I had learned my brother, Bradley, was diagnosed with Duchene Muscular Dystrophy. I did not know much about it, but I knew that it was a disease and that it would harm my brother. How long he will be here is not definite, so I have learned to appreciate life a little more. Do not take life for granted because no one knows when their last day on this earth will be. Until your life or someone else's has been threatened to be taken away, you cannot understand the capacity of that statement.

Duchene Muscular Dystrophy is a disease that affects the muscles of the body, usually in boys. The disease is progressive, which means that the disease will gradually get worse. Doctors say that people with this disease will stop walking by the age of twelve, but by the inferences I have made, there is not a definite time they will stop walking. I have seen boys that are nine years old and in wheelchairs. I have also heard about boys as old as fifteen, and still walking. My brother is thirteen and still walking. I think that you have to want to keep walking in order to maintain the ability to, but I know that because of steroids, stretches, and leg braces, Bradley is still able to walk. Walking is not the only ability that boys, and sometimes girls, lose. They also lose the use of their arms and hands. Breathing is made difficult for them and their heart does not pump as well. Those who cannot breathe well are put on ventilators. There are many medications that can help with all of these symptoms, but there is no known cure.

In the year of 2001, Bradley was diagnosed with Duchene Muscular Dystrophy. He was 3 years old. My mom and dad knew, before then, that something was not right. When Bradley had learned to walk, it was difficult for him to go up hills. He would walk and run like his hip was out of place. Most of the time, you would find him crawling. He would also have many falls and in order to get back up, he would try to hold on to something or proceed to get on all fours and push himself up.

My mom went to many doctors in order to figure out what was wrong. She went to the family doctor, chiropractor, and pediatrician;, none of which knew what was wrong. My dad suggested my mom go to Doctor Alexander, who was on the board at the bank where my dad worked. He agreed that something was wrong. My mom took Bradley to physical therapy. The physical therapist said that Bradley had muscle weakness. Mom mentioned it to the chiropractor and she said that Bradley had large calves, which was a sign of Muscular Dystrophy. Mom went to the physical therapist again and the therapist said that she thought that it was Muscular Dystrophy, too. Mom thought it was crazy but researched Muscular Dystrophy herself. She felt that she was reading about Bradley because he had every symptom the paper explained. She went back to Doctor Alexander and he referred us to Saint Louis Children's Hospital.

We took Bradley to the hospital and we met Doctor Neil in November of 2000. He wanted to run a creatinine phosphokinase. (CPK) It is a blood test that determines muscle damage by the amount of CPK leaking into the blood. A normal CPK ranges from zero to 250. Bradley's was 14,000. That alone told us that Bradley had Muscular Dystrophy, but he would have to have a biopsy in order to confirm it. In January of 2001, the test came back positive for Duchene Muscular Dystrophy.

In November of 2000, I learned that my brother had the disease, even though he had not had a biopsy. The doctor was sure because of the very high CPK. It just so happened that we got the phone call from the doctor at night about the CPK levels. I went into the kitchen, where my mom was cooking supper, and saw that she was crying. I asked, "Mommy, why are you crying?" She told me that Bradley had Muscular Dystrophy. I did not know how to react, and one of my statements proved this. Bradley came into the kitchen and I jokingly said, "Bradley, you're gonna die." This statement made my mom upset and I felt bad.

Sometimes the quote repeats in my head over and over again. I regret saying it, but I was seven and too young to fully understand what was going on with my brother. Now, I know there is some truth to that statement, which makes me feel even worse. Guilt ran through my head that night. All I could think about was that maybe I had played with him too roughly, but my mom assured me that it was not that, and that some diseases are genetic. It was a lot to take in, but now that I am older, I know what Duchene Muscular Dystrophy is so well that I could write about it in a magazine if I wanted to.

I felt somewhat sad that night, but I do not think it was to the level of my mom's sadness. I have always been empathetic, so I was sad to see my mother cry. I knew that my father was sad, but I did not see it from him physically. I assume he was hiding it, maybe to stay strong for our family. My brother was too young to understand but, I feel like he knew that he had a disease and that it would harm him. I think that seeing everyone's reaction showed me how serious my brother's condition was. It also pulled our family closer.

As I think about it now, there really is no place or time you find out these things. Sad times come when they want to. I know exactly where I was and how I felt. I was in my kitchen standing by the oven. I could pin point the area for anyone who came to my house and asked. I will never forget it because it has changed my family's life so much.

As I grew older, there were points in my life when I felt angry at God. How could He allow my family to go through so much pain? I have learned that God has a plan for my brother's life, though. Everything happens for a reason. It does not mean that I should be happy that my brother has a disease, but that I should be happy for what God has done for Bradley. He is doing so well and I am surprised that he can still walk. It is truly a miracle. Doctors are surprised, too.

Now, we go to Cincinnati's Children's Hospital. They are one of the best hospitals in the United States. The doctors there provide such great care and we are very lucky to have them. There is always good and there is bad news, but they work to change the bad news. They do not just care for their patients; they also care for the family. That was good for me, because at other hospitals I felt ignored as the sister.

A Geneticist came and talked to me at the hospital in Cincinnati and asked if I wanted to take a test to determine whether or not I was a carrier. I agreed to take it and, unfortunately, the test came back positive. I was upset, but if I have a child with the same disease as my brother, I will know how to take care of the child. Sometimes you have to look for the positive things in a negative circumstance. Since my brother has a disease, it has encouraged me to become a nurse, which is another positive thing that has come from this.

Life is not always going to be easy. There are sad and trying times, but it is the sad and trying times that show who we really are. Do not allow these times get you down. Always stay positive. Do not take life for granted because you really do not know when your last day is. Live your life to the fullest even when you get the bad news.

Stephanie Jones (Bradley's sister)

Josiah, 13 And Cody, 17

Cody walked today. His steps were few and very calculated. He struggled so desperately to let each foot rise and again come to rest on the floor beneath him. My eyes filled with tears of great joy and yet sadness. My beloved child before me fought so diligently to obtain some strength in his dying muscles. This was a good day, I reasoned, within myself. Cody walked. He took steps, no matter how few. Some were better than none. But by comparison to what? Each day more fear grows inside of me as I become his legs and arms. Alone, I watch this beautiful child lose himself to a disease that shows no mercy and strips away all hope . While I smile at him now and sing praise to the five steps he took, my heart breaks in silence. Later within the walls of my own room, my tears of the sorrow yet to come will flood me. I will cry. I will face my greatest fear and challenges. Alone, I will pull myself up and out of the darkness I feel and be all that my beautiful children need. Through shaking hands and sobs of heart-felt pain and loss, I will carry Cody forward.

Josiah pulled himself up from the floor today. Though it took much assurance that he could do it, he finally raised himself to a standing position. It took so much for my little one to make his weakening muscles allow him to stand, his eyes showing the enormous strength he puts forward into such a simple task for most of us. I rejoice in tears. He managed a task Cody no longer can. We embrace to celebrate another moment of victory. Inside, I feel torn and experience fear growing. Reasoning again, I know this is a good day. Josiah stood by himself. When the day ends, again I will cry alone my tears of loss, then find comfort by remembering moments of a time when life felt different. For now, I will enjoy Josiah and celebrate all his abilities. We will take one day at a time. My fear and sorrow I will hide today. I will be strong for Josiah. I will be the muscle he needs.

While I fight my own fears and search for courage, I pray that I can be strong enough to never let Josiah and Cody feel alone. I know I must put all their needs first and be the forces they will need to get through each day. While holding back my tears, I will have to dry theirs. To help them face each day with courage, I will have to hide my fears. Even though I walk alone at times, I will have to let them know I will be with them always. As the sun rises tomorrow, so shall we, together.

Rita Zondio Felling

Ansel

Excerpt from Moonrise ~Penny Wolfson - I Falling, 1998

I am at the Grand Union in Dobbs Ferry, New York, with my son Ansel, who is thirteen years old. It's raining. He begged to come, so I brought him, not really wanting to, because I had to bring his wheelchair, too: it weighs more than two hundred pounds and isn't easy to maneuver into the minivan, even with the ramp. I have to wrestle the motorized chair unit it faces forward and then, bending and squeezing into the narrow confines of the van, I have to fasten it to the floor with several clasps. By the time I have done this even once, I'm irritable. A trip to the supermarket means doing it twice and undoing it twice.

Anyway, we've finished our shopping, and we leave the supermarket. Ansel is in his chair, without his hooded yellow raincoat is babyish, not cool. He's afraid people at school will laugh at him. Maybe it's true, I say, but I think it's stupid. Why get wet when you can stay dry? Needless to say, I lose this argument.

Before loading the groceries I open the van door so that Ansel can get in the front seat, where he always sits if Joe isn't with us. He parks his chair at a distance from the minivan, so that I'll have room for the ramp, and starts to rise, laboriously. No. "Rise" sounds too easy, like smoke going up a flue, airy, like yeast bread rising in the oven. Ansel does not rise. He shifts sideways in the seat and pulls himself up heavily, propping his eighty pounds against the armrest for balance. He leans with his left arm, twists his right shoulder around to straighten up, and brings his hip and buttocks to a partly standing position. Actually, he's sort of bent in half, with his hands still on the chair's joystick. There is a moment of imbalance. His feet are planted far apart, farther out than his hips, and he needs to bounce back and forth a few times to bring his feet together. Finally he's up. He begins walking toward the door in his waddling, tiptoe way. His spine is curved quite a bit from scoliosis, his stomach is forward, his hands are out at his sides chest-high, his fingers outstretched.

His balance is so tenuous that his five-year-old brother, Toby, can knock him down. Sometimes Ansel will bellow, "I'm tired of everyone always leaving things all over the floor! Don't they know I'll fall?" It's true that we're a little careless about this. But Ansel will trip over anything--an unevenness in the sidewalk, the dog's water dish, some bits of food on the floor, things expected and unexpected--and sometimes over nothing. Sooner or later he falls. It's part of the routine. And the older he gets, the more he falls.

Now in Grand Union parking lot, he falls. Who know why--it could be the wet ground. He's in the skinny aisle of asphalt between our car and the one parked next to us. He falls, and it's pouring, and I'm still loading the grocery bags into the back.

"MOM!" he calls at me, half barking, half crying. "I fell!" There's such anguish, such anger, in his voice when he falls, and such resignation. He never thinks I hear him.

And why am I suddenly angry? Such terrible impatience rises in me now. Am I really such a witch, such a bad mother, that when I'm loading groceries and my son falls, I don't have the time or patience to cope? Why am I so angry

"Wait a minute," I say. "I'll be there in a minute."

So he sits on the wet pavement between the cars. I know his sweatpants are at this moment soaking through. I can see that the wheelchair, waiting to be rolled up the ramp, needing to be pushed and yanked into position, is also getting wet. Its foamy nylon seat will need drying out later.

A middle-aged, blond woman has wheeled her shopping cart into the lot and approaches us. "Can I help?"

No, you definitely cannot help, runs through my head. This is both true and self-righteous. Physically, the job is not meant for two; it's easier for me to do on my own. How would we two, and Ansel, even fit between the cars?

I grit my teeth and smile and say, "No, no thanks, really. I can do it." People always seem puzzled and upset when they see him fall. It's so sudden, an instant crumpling, without warning. They can't see the weakness, the steady deterioration of his pelvis. Maybe someone would fall this way if he'd been hit hard in the solar plexus; I don't know. But Ansel's feet give way for no apparent reason, and he's down.

The blond woman has heard me, but she keeps standing there, her hands clamped around the handle of her cart, her eyes moving from Ansel to the grocery bags to me. I know she means to be helpful, and in a way I do want something from her –pity? An acknowledgment that I am more noble than she? But mostly I want her to go away. *Don't look at me. Don't watch this.*

"Mom! Where are you?"

I turn from the blond woman; she fades away. "OK, I'm coming," I say. I try to wedge myself between the cars so that I can retrieve Ansel. There's a special way to pick him up: you have to come from behind and grab him under his arms, raise him so that his toes dangle just above the ground, and then set his feet down precisely the right distance apart.

I'm in pretty good shape, but Ansel is dead weight. Another child could help you, could put his arms around your neck. His feet would come off the ground at even the suggestion of lifting. But Ansel is pulling me down, his limp shoulders, his heavy leg braces, his sodden pants, his clumsy sneakers. I can't hold him. My own sneakers slip on the wet pavement.

Penny Wolfson
Moonrise

Ryan, 13 Years Old

It was early Monday morning when the phone rang. My husband answered it. It was the doctor and she wanted to talk with me. I had taken Ryan to see the doctor on Friday. He had been complaining of being tired a lot and I noticed that, at almost 5 yrs old, he was having a hard time keeping up with other kids his age. She said she wanted to do some blood work. I didn't think anything more about it. On the phone that Monday morning I listened with unbelief as she told me that Ryan's CK count came back extremely high. She said that meant he had Muscular Dystrophy. She continued on to say that we had to confirm the diagnosis with a DNA blood test but there was no hurry because DMD has no treatment or cure. She told us she didn't have much information and suggested we look on the internet. After hearing the news ,I sat down in my living room floor. I couldn't speak when my husband asked me what the doctor said. When I finally told him, we both just sat there, stunned and silent. It was the furthest things from our mind. We had no idea whatsoever. It was a complete and unexpected shock and we were taken completely by surprise.

Ryan's diagnosis was confirmed a few months later. Up until that point, we could hope, hope that she was wrong, hope that the blood tests were wrong, and hope that it was something else. The results from the DNA were confirmed; we were once again silent. Ryan is my youngest of 4 boys and the only one affected by DMD. When we were told that he had this disease that has no treatment or cure and 100% death rate, we experienced a death. We felt the loss of what we thought was a healthy child. Our hopes for his future, the dreams we had for him, the thoughts of what his life would be like were forever changed at that point. We grieved the loss of what was not to be.

The grieving and mourning process when you have a child with DMD is not a onetime thing. With each "loss" Ryan experienced, no longer able to run, ride a bike, walk across the room, dress himself, to walk, the loss of innocence when he comes home from camp and with tears in his eyes asks you if he is going to die young, to see the look on his face when an unthinking doctor says he will have to have back surgery because without it he will become like a pretzel and his internal organs will be crushed, you grieve again, and again. There has been no end to the grieving and mourning process. I just get to where I have accepted the loss and being okay with where Ryan is, and then he declines some more and the process starts all over again. It has not gotten any easier. In fact, each loss has gotten harder and harder to accept. I am often on the verge of tears yet have to put on a brave front for Ryan's sake. Not only am I trying to deal with it but I have to help Ryan deal with it. It is very wearing and emotionally and physically draining.

I know this isn't the same as an actual death but, in a way, it is. It took me a long time to realize that this emotional roller-coaster I was experiencing was a grieving, mourning process. Knowing that doesn't make it any easier and doesn't stop me from going through it. I wish there was a way to deal with this without having to go through that process. I have, at least I feel that I have, given Ryan over to God and trust Him. Still my heart hurts.

These things are hard to talk about; in fact, I haven't shared these feelings with very many people. I know Ryan's disease is not easy to hear about, and I don't think most people would understand or really want to know. Most people's knowledge of DMD is that Jerry Lewis has a telethon every Labor Day. It is easier to ignore that it is going on than to have to deal with it. In fact, that is how my husband has dealt with it until recently. He had not wanted to face the facts. When he was in the Air Force, he was away from home a lot and didn't have to deal with it. Since recently changing jobs, he has been home, and he has had to face the reality of the situation. He had stuffed his feelings and didn't want to talk about it. He isolated himself and kept very busy with work so he didn't have to deal with things. He became angry and bitter towards God and even his family Thankfully, he is now working through these feelings and is learning how to deal with things a little better.

Working through the grieving/mourning process over and over again is very much part of DMD life. Even though we go through this, we realize that our life on earth is just a blink of the eye and that one day Ryan will leave his wheelchair behind here on earth and will walk—no, RUN--for all of eternity in heaven. No boundaries of disease will hold him back and, because of that, we once again have hope.

Donna Mckenzie

Ryan

I sit and watch as you walk by,
thinking perhaps to catch your eye.
My legs are weak and my arms are too,
and I'd like to stand up tall as you.
But, for now, as you can see,
it would be nice if you came to me.
Kneel down and you will see;
there IS a someone like you ... Inside of me!!

Ryan says that he sometimes feels invisible. People just walk past him or avoid looking at him. I don't think you have to be in a wheelchair to feel this way .There are so many people around us that are hurting. I guess what Ryan has taught me is to NOT look past people but to be open to "see" them, really see. I think that having a child with Duchene has opened my eyes to things I probably wouldn't have noticed before.

We live near an Army base and, few weeks ago, Ryan and I went to the food court on the Post to eat lunch. I ordered our food and then proceeded to find a place to sit. It was so crowded that we just stood there looking around. There were a few tables in the middle of the room but, with Ryan's wheelchair, we couldn't get to them. As Ryan asked me where we were going to sit, a Soldier came up to me and asked me if we needed a place to sit. I said yes. He then proceeded to go back to his table where his friend was sitting. He picked up his food, which he hadn't finished yet, and said, "You can have our table." I thanked him and sat down, but, as I was eating, I was fighting back tears. I kept thinking about what he did, just a small act of kindness right? So why was it making me want to cry. Well, later, as I was thinking about it, I realized why it touched my heart so much. He SAW us! We weren't invisible to him!

Mary Huffman (Ryan's grandma)

Callam, 13 Years Old

We humans were made for eternity. Maybe you believe that when we die, that's it. Or maybe you believe we're learning to live eternally with God. Maybe you're not sure. But whatever you think about our fate, in each of us there's a yearning to matter, to make a difference. For something good about us to go on. For eternity. For many of us, that's in the form of our children.

And that's what this story is about.

Jolie got the first glimpse of eternity. During her pregnancy with Callam, she had a dream where an aide at her school appeared to tell her that God needed angels in heaven, and then flew away with Callam. The dream was on her mind the next day when the very same person approached to give her a gift, a beautiful set of angel figurines holding babies. Jolie was so stunned that the poor girl stepped back in shock, fearing she had done something wrong. It was a lightning bolt for a 39-year-old mom who worked every day with special-needs kids. Jolie knew she was on notice for something.

Alan got a glimpse, too. If there was ever a star first-born, who enjoyed five years of Mom and Dad's undivided attention, Savannah was it. Bright, precociously verbal, a voracious reader by preschool, in many ways an old soul in a child's body, Savannah was a delight beyond words. During a Thanksgiving Eve church service about the same time, while giving thanks for the blessing of a healthy, happy child in Savannah, Alan was gripped with a sense that it shouldn't be taken for granted, and that he should pray, specifically, not for good circumstances, but for faith in facing something that was going to be really, really tough. Shivers down the back.

Eternity is a strange thing. We're not really equipped for it. We know how to live one day at a time. In fact, living that way is often seen as a key to happiness.

But sometimes, a rogue wave washes us overboard into that endless sea of eternity. Maybe we're devastated by the death or betrayal of a loved one. Maybe we realize how we've hurt someone, and that we can't do anything to change it. Or maybe we learn that our child has a disease that will gradually destroy his body and ultimately take his life.

At six months of pregnancy, the docs could identify the symptom but not the cause. They had a name for it, though: "idiopathic polyhydramnios." Polyhydramnios means "too much amniotic fluid," and "idiopathic," literally is Latin for "uncertain cause," or in common English "we don't know why." Jolie had what looked like a full-term pregnancy at about 6 months. She didn't balloon up all over. She just looked like she was about to pop with a baby. In retrospect, it was perfect preparation for raising a special-needs child. Complete strangers would ask her, "When are you due?" When she would tell them, they would say sensitive, supporting things like, "Holy crap! You look like you're about to have it right here!"

With all that extra room, Callam had a big time in there, so much that when he came out he had the cord wrapped tightly around his neck, 3 times. Scared the crap out of Dad, but he was OK. Ironic, isn't it? A Duchenne kid almost strangling himself turning flips.

Bobbing up and down in that sea of eternity, we're no longer facing isolated facts, events that come to us in single file down the railroad tracks of time. We're immersed in non-negotiable, inarguable Truth. Over our heads in eternity, with no idea which way to swim.

Moms know when something isn't right, and as Callam grew, Jolie knew exactly that. He was smart, alert, extremely inquisitive, but mostly stationary. His favorite thing as a crawler was to gather his toys in a circle on the floor around him, within arm's reach, and methodically destroy them. His favorite thing in the world was to disassemble something. Even at that pre-verbal age, "What's inside it?" and "How does it work?" were his chief concerns. Dad once actually saw him looking long and inquisitively at his own forearm; it seemed that he wanted to twist it off at the elbow, to have a look inside and see how it worked.

When we're young and vigorous, ready to go and see and do, we always think we're ready. Whatever the question, the answer is "Yes! Right now!" Garrison Keillor tells a story from his childhood of overhearing his parents discuss whether to let him attend the funeral of an elderly relatively. " I just think it's too much," he recalls his mother saying, and he recalls of his small-town upbringing, at that point, Too Much sounded just about perfect.

He never ran. Oh, he ran a few feet, a few times at Mom and Dad's worried urging, but he never just ran the way little boys do. He never once hopped or jumped with both feet off the floor. He never climbed on the bars at preschool, though in one superhuman burst he climbed to the top of a McDonald's playland and then wailed like a wounded penguin when he couldn't get down through the maze. Dad had to go up in there after him. Lesson: if you weigh more than 200 pounds, the McDonald's playland is not designed for you.

Moses thought that Too Much sounded just about perfect, too. He was an old man in body, but remarkably young in spirit. On Mt. Sinai he begged God, "Let me see you!" but God shook His head. "Too much," He said. "You literally wouldn't survive it. The best I can do is to let you see my back, to see where I've been, what I've done." He was right, of course. Moses came back down the mountain shaken, ready to change the world, his face literally glowing from an experience so and terrifying he couldn't possibly express it.

And then he saw some asshole parking in a handicapped spot.

So began the season of frustration. What was going on with our little boy? The first step was getting someone in authority to see it. Lots of pats on the head. He's just developmentally delayed, idiopathically. He'll grow out of it.

To be fair, pediatricians have a tough job, and calming worried parents has to be a never-ending part of it. Doctors are taught, "When you hear hoofbeats, think horses, not zebras." That means that the simplest explanation is usually the right one. Every parent is convinced that if their kid is not a prodigy, he must have some terrible, rare disease. But here's the thing: *Some of them do.*

Becoming a big sister was big fun for Savannah. For about ten minutes, until Callam literally pooped on her the first time she held him. He's been delighted by that story his whole life; she is much less amused. But it could hardly have been more appropriate to the story. By this time Savannah was about ten, naturally developing her own identity among her peers at school. In her delightful world of reading Harry Potter and writing fan-fiction, making new friends and learning new skills, Mom and Dad were psychologically working double shifts, woefully distracted, struggling to think of anything but "Who will listen to us? Who can tell us what's wrong with our little boy?" Savannah slowly began to realize that she was going to have to make her own way, that nothing would be the same, and, in retrospect, that realization began a long, understandable struggle with resentment, capped with the subsequent news that she was a carrier. A lot for a ten-year old to handle. She has handled it like the astonishingly mature kids she's been since birth. She grew up fast, because she had to. But she has suffered like everybody else in this story.

We waited six months to get into a pediatric neurologist, who looked at him for five minutes and said, literally, "He's a floppy kid. Floppy muscles. He'll grow out of it." Idiopathically, right? Thanks, Doc.

Jolie is an educator and saw things through an educator's eyes. Since the docs couldn't see it, she turned to the school model. She applied to have Callam tested for special-needs preschool, hoping to get some services, some insight, anything to validate what she was seeing. But at the school district, it was the blind leading the blind.

"Well, it says here that he's above-normal intelligence and verbal acuity." Yep. Did you actually talk to him for three minutes him before you gave him that test? Maybe you could have saved some time. By the way, did you watch him walk? "It says here that if you miss three on the psych eval, you're prone to depression, so we'll put that down." Really? He's four years old. You think he can't get up off the floor because he's depressed?

"We noticed he's started stuttering." Yeah, we noticed that too. Maybe it's because he's frustrated with you morons treating him like a science fair project.

"He won't climb the monkey bars." This was the worst, from the physical therapist. Not "can't," but "won't. Because he's willfully defiant and has it in for me personally. " Right. It's about you. A four year-old boy has never kept up with this peers on the playground because he's determined to make you look bad. And whose development was arrested?

After much eye-rolling, he was dismissed from the special-needs pre-school program because, well, he didn't fit any of the standard categories, so clearly, he didn't have any special needs. On to gen-ed kindergarten.

By now, Callam was having noticeable difficulty walking, with an awkward gait, thrusting his chest out, head back, with a strange flopping tippy-toe gait. He struggled to step up on curbs and labored to the point of agony on a flight of stairs, literally pulling himself up with the handrail. And he had adopted this curious strategy to get up from the floor...

His kindergarten teacher called us before noon on the first day of school. "I'm really worried about him," she said. "We tried to go up the stairs and he couldn't do it at all. I think we need to meet..." Bless you. By the time we met, a different school PT had spent some time with Callam and knew the score. Of course ,she couldn't diagnose him, but she urged us to ask the neurologist whether Callam had "some sort of dystrophy."

There was that word. Dad went home and googled it, saw an exact description of Callam, read the life-expectancy part, said "Wow, I'm glad that's not it," and shut off the computer.

It was months before we got back in to see the neurologist, but we weren't there five minutes before, while he was looking at the blood work results, he saw Callam out of the corner of his eye, getting up from the floor in a classic Gower's sign maneuver. The doctor went pale, eyes darting to the CPK numbers on the sheet, actually mouthing "No..."

And so the evil wave knocked us into the sea of eternity, as if we were nothing but empty cardboard boxes on the deck. Like Moses, we're not ready for eternity.

Bobbing up and down, trying to find bottom under our feet, not knowing where to turn, what to ask, whom to talk to. Who holds our hand? Who shows us the way to go?

Notice it's "show," the way, not "tell." Not "point." Nowadays, we're connected with hundreds of Duchenne families from all over the English-speaking world (and even a few non-English speakers!). But in those pre-Facebook days? In those first months, we lurched from one thing to another. We didn't trust ourselves: we didn't know anything about this. So we did whatever the so-called professionals told us to do. They know what they're doing, right? They have degrees on the walls!

We got so much bad advice, yelling in our ears from every direction. Tough love! That was the name of the endless unspoken song, every verse another variation on the theme, "Don't you dare fail as a parent, especially of this special child!"

"Make him stand in the standing frame, even if he screams! Make him walk! He has to walk 'til he's twelve! Stretch his heel cords, every night, without fail! The insurance company must have absolute confirmation that it's Duchenne: let's cut a hole in one of his major muscles. That's what it says in my outdated textbook. Look, see here? "

Yeah, maybe we should bleed him with leeches while we're at it.

Ask anyone who lives with a debilitating medical condition and they'll tell you the same thing: it brings out the best in most people and the absolute worst in a few. This reached its absolute low point about a year and a half after Callam's diagnosis, when his first-grade teacher concluded that her inability to engage him couldn't be her failure as a teacher; it had to be Mom and Dad's fault. The poor kid doesn't just have this terrible disease; he has these lazy bums for parents. Based on lie after lie, this evil wretch sent both the police and CPS to our house, in the hopes that they would remove Callam (in both cases, the officials stepped in our house, looked around, and asked "Why are we here? Did you piss somebody off?")

Looking back, it's impossible not to get angry at all of that. In fact, anger is the perfect response, because we had to get angry to see Truth. When it came to Callam, the so-called experts had the luxury of specialization. They were dealing with facts at their leisure, one at a time. They were on the ship, leaning over the rail, yelling conflicting instructions, while we bobbed in the sea of eternity, treading water furiously, trying to balance the central, everyday conflict of this disease:

"How do we help our son enjoy this precious day for what it is, while not giving up on what his future days can be?"

Eight years into this, we still don't have a clear answer to that. We struggle with the constant tradeoff of effort versus exhaustion. We struggle to balance the risk of exposing him to infection versus his joy at being with his friends, of meeting Callam's needs while not burning out ourselves as his caregivers. We struggle to balance Savannah's needs with Callam's.

Eternity is still Way Way Too Much. But when we think about the precious gift of these two children, about the honor of being their parents, about their special gits, their insights, their tender hearts and zeal for what's right, we begin to see exactly where God has been. He's been right here the whole time.

Alan and Jolie Thomas

Francis Douglas Desmond, 12 Years Old

Our names are Steven and Suzanne Desmond. We were married September 10, 1994, and are proud parents of three beautiful children, Francis, age 12, Lucas age 10, and Zoey, age 7. We live in Orchard Park, New York, a town roughly 20 minutes outside of Buffalo, New York. The following story is about our eldest son, Francis, who has been diagnosed with Duchenne Muscular Dystrophy. This is a hard thing to speak about, but we must if we are ever going to get the answers we are looking for.

On Sunday, August 9, 1998, at 8:20 p.m., a beautiful baby boy was born weighing 7 lbs., 12 oz. We named him Francis Douglas Desmond. Francis was named after three people, his fraternal grandfather, Douglas Vincent Desmond; his maternal grandfather, Eugene Francis Weimer; and his father, Steven Douglas Desmond. He was a happy and good-natured baby and he reached all expected milestones, like walking shortly after his 1 year birthday. We had all the hopes and dreams that any parent would have for their child, but little did we know that at age 3, two bricks would enter our lives that would shatter the dreams we had for his life.

The family noticed that, at age 3, Francis was falling behind. He did not talk like other children, wanted things in a certain way and isolated himself a lot. When our school district's special education department tested him, they found that he had delayed development across the board. When he was 3½, we immediately got him enrolled in a special education pre-school. Try putting a 3-year-old on the bus is not fun. They think you're giving them away, and that's what it felt like. Thank God for his little brother Lucas, who was a baby at the time That meant I had someone to take care of for Francis' first day of school. After taking the bus ride to and from school, he started to enjoy the rides, but that didn't make it easier for us.

At age 4, Francis' school physical therapist became concerned about him. He suggested that we see a neurologist. We did our research and got him an appointment. The doctor examined him and at the second visit told us that Francis might have something called Duchenne Muscular Dystrophy (DMD). After a lifetime of watching the Jerry Lewis MDA Telethon, I knew there was no cure for DMD. But I did not know enough about it to know what was in his future or what lay ahead.

For the next four years, Steve and I were frozen in fear and denial. We felt like we were in quick sand and, if we made a slight move, everything would crash to the ground. I have so much respect for parents who just dive in and get to work, but some of us take a little longer, I guess. We kept telling Francis to walk on his heals until, one day, he could not do it anymore, no matter how much he tried. In the fall of 2006, we started talking about our feelings, about what medical condition Francis might have. We decided that we needed to know the answer, positive or negative. We had to know for his sake. We went for a second opinion and on January 3, 2007, at the age of 8, Francis was diagnosed with Duchenne Muscular Dystrophy (DMD) with a mutation called HEMIZYGOUS IVS55-IG>C Mutation. On that day, the lives of everyone in our family changed forever. At least we knew that we had a better chance of fighting this uninvited monster that had entered our lives. We began doing as much research as we could and still do that today.

Francis is currently being seen by a neurologist at Cincinnati Children's Hospital Medical Center in Cincinnati, Ohio, under the care of Dr. Brenda Wong, who works only with patients that have Duchenne and Becker Muscular Dystrophy. He is currently on Deflazacort (steroid) to slow down the progression of DMD, Fosamax to keep his bones healthy and to prevent osteoporosis, Losartan to protect his heart, and several vitamins, for example, extra calcium.

We have built a handicap accessible bedroom and bathroom off of our living room on the first floor so he does not have climb the stairs anymore. He loves his new room!

Some boys just have DMD, and I would not wish that on my worst enemy, but Francis also has a learning disability/challenge. Due to this, he has been in special education classes since the age of 3. My husband takes photos for an organization here in Buffalo called Gliding Stars Adaptive Ice Skating Programs. I volunteer, as well as Lucas and Zoey, and we teach the mentally and physically challenged to ice skate. Every year we hold an ice show to celebrate the skaters' accomplishments on the ice._www.glidingstars.org._ It was started by a wonderful woman and, in my book, a hero, Elizabeth O'Donnell. Francis was a star/skater beginning when he was 5, but due to the progression of and weakness from DMD, he stopped skating in 2008. While other skaters got stronger due to skating, he grew weaker due to his DMD, but, at the same time, it was a great experience. And wearing the skates helped with his heel cords. When he was 9, he won an award for his efforts in skating as well as for his improved attitude. He was so proud of himself when he received it.

Because I'm an instructor at Gliding Stars, I see a lot of different challenges that people have. In 2007-2008, I really noticed that Frances had a challenge that was undeniable. All along I felt his school was not acknowledging it. After nine months of waiting, I made an appointment with a neuro-psychologist and, in August, 2008, at the age of 10, Francis was diagnosed with Autism Spectrum Disorder (ASD), only to have the school not agree with the diagnosis. I felt their denial of his disorder set Francis up for a very bad school year in 2008-2009. With that behind us though, he now goes to a wonderful school called Autistic Services, Inc. It's a school for children diagnosed with ASD. They are giving him the help he needs and deserves. Age ten is a late diagnosis for Autism. I wish I had recognized it sooner so he could have gotten help for it sooner. I know this book is for raising awareness for DMD, but I would also like to raise awareness that a certain percentage of these boys have challenges other than just the DMD.

Like Francis, they can also have ASD. The medical community must acknowledge everything concerning a patient with DMD because, in some cases, there is a lot more going on than just the DMD. So, the whole patient should be taken care of. If there is no one at the neurologist's office who can help with these other conditions, the family should be given a reference to someone who can help. The point is to treat the whole patient, not just the disease. Everyday I see Francis fight not only with his body, but with his mind as well. When he isolated himself before the age of 3, when he needed things a certain way or even lined up his Thomas the Train Engines, put his hot wheels cars in certain order and exhibited some bad behaviors like hitting, yelling and being destructive to property, little did we know that these were signs of his Autism.

I have never been tested to know if I am a carrier for DMD, but I feel strongly that something went wrong at conception on the X chromosome. Yes, it's a genetic disease, but what is scary is that it can occur in children with no family history of the disease. There are even some girls who have DMD, although it's very rare.

Francis is a smart, fun, happy, giving, thoughtful and beautiful 12-year-old boy with a smile that lights up a room. He deserves more than DMD and Autism. We are blessed that, at age twelve, he is still able to walk and does not take for granted that other boys his age are in a wheelchair. Like I said earlier, Francis has a Splice Site Mutation HEMIZYGOUS IVS55-IG>C Mutation. According to Baylor College in Texas, Francis' particular Splice Site Mutation is the only one ever recorded. We don't know whether to be scared or grateful for this.

While watching the Jerry Lewis MDA Telethon all my life, I never dreamed that I would have a son that would become one of Jerry's Kids. Thank God we have people such as Jerry Lewis. I would love to meet him someday if given the chance! I don't know what people before him and others like him did to lead the way, like a wonderful lady by the name of Pat Furlong of Ohio, who started Parent Project Muscular Dystrophy. Parent Project is a wonderful resource for families with a member diagnosed with

DMD/BMD. www.parentprojectmd.org_Pat lost two sons to DMD at age 15 and 17 and continues her fight against DMD in honor of her late sons and to help other families affected by this disease. We love you, Pat! We no longer have to feel alone. If we all work together for these boys and men, we have hope. I have made connections with other families, not only in western New York, but all over the country and the world. We all help each other not only learn about treatments and physical therapy, but also and, most importantly, we help each other cope with all the emotions that go along with this diagnosis of DMD.

Even though Francis has these issues in his life and even though it hurts so much to see him go through things at times, he still finds a reason to smile. That's what keeps us going, not only for him, but for our family. We will never give up hope that a cure will someday be found. We kept this private for a long time but know now that awareness and raising funds for research are the way to getting the help that these boys and men need and deserve. We love you, we will always be here for you, Francis, and we will never stop fighting for you.

With all my love and may God Bless you,

Suzanne M. Desmond
Francis' Mother
Photograph by Desmond's Focus Photography: Steven D. Desmond

SECTION III
The Late Phase: Breath and the Beating Heart

Fifty or even twenty years ago, the life expectancy of Duchenne boys was between 14-16. Now with new discoveries about respiratory preservation and oxidative stress management, more boys are living well into adulthood, some even reaching their thirties, rarely their forties, but it is heard of.

Now the child/adult with Duchenne is pretty much paralyzed. Some boys can move a little bit; however, they are completely physically dependent on someone else to care for their daily hygiene needs as well as dressing, feeding and pretty much anything that requires any kind of strength. These demanding needs usually fall upon the parent. This, in turn, takes a toll on finances, especially if it is a single parent household. There are agencies to provide personal care but funding is limited.

Things can go from bad to worse in a blink of an eye, even deadly. This phase forces the serious side of facing death, with medical choices of tracheotomy (a surgical operation creating an opening or hole into the trachea--the front of the neck--so a tube can be inserted to assist breathing), and heart treatment plans. Some patients and families choose to take their chances, while others will go for it. Either way, this period of waiting for the other shoe to drop is intense but at the same time can be rewarding in the respect the child and parent's relationship is magnified. Often times the parent is the only one who understands.

If the Duchenne boy lives to see his high school graduation, enormous feelings of mixed triumph, relief and fear are a constant battle. They made it, beaten up by Duchenne, but they've made it. Now what?

What about college or just living another day? All the parents want is for their child to be happy and live a quality of life, for however long they can.

Dusty, 18 Years Old

The Dark Cloud of Duchenne

I once read that life isn't about waiting for the storm to pass but learning how to dance in the rain. The diagnosis of Duchenne muscular dystrophy felt like a sharp sword that stabbed and shattered my world.

After that moment, a dark cloud hovered above my head and would never leave. Every time I looked up, there it was, reminding me of the perils that lay before me. It was a frightening time, to think that my perfect, sweet child of six, whom I loved with all my heart, was going to progressively get weaker, until he could no longer walk or use his arms. He would lose his ability to eat or breathe on his own, and on top of all that, his life expectancy was put at age 20, if he was lucky to live that long. I felt an anguish that only a mother could understand, and my world stopped. How was I to navigate through this mess? There was no cure for my son, and no treatments. What was this disease? What did it all mean? What about my other children? The dark cloud was all around me. That was 11 years ago. To say there have been many challenges over the years is clearly an understatement. My earlier pursuits of undergraduate and graduate degrees were nothing compared to the task at hand. Not only did my husband and I have to learn about the complexities of Duchenne, but we also had to become experts in a short amount of time in order to fully understand and comprehend this disease if we were to save our son.

As we embarked upon this endeavor, we would learn the language of doctors and specialists and enter a world of genetics: DNA, RNA, dystro-phin, utrophin. We conversed with scientists and discussed with neurologists, orthopedists, cardiologists, and pulmonologists, and even pharmaceutical companies. The list went on and on.

We had to educate family, friends, teachers, schools, physical therapists, and attend conferences. We became lobbyists, organized fundraisers, and served on charities. Eventually we would have to research wheelchairs and adaptive technologies and later assistive devices, such as coughing and breathing machines.

Over the years, difficult decisions were made regarding drug treatments. The side effects of some of the drugs, such as cortico-steroids, were dramatic. Another, gentamycin, also generated toxic side effects. But there was little else. Further along we learned about a small molecule drug and participated in a very promising drug trial. My son was poked and biopsied and became a guinea pig for the generations to come after him. It turned out that, for 18 months, he was on a dose that was actually ineffective. The trial stopped temporarily.

Throughout, the dark cloud remained. My son was getting weaker, and, despite all we were doing, we had little choice but slowly to surrender to the relentless nature of Duchenne, which was steadily stealing his life away. Although there have been huge advances with the unveiling of new drug trials, and many scientists coming forward with renewed optimism and hope, today there is still no cure for my son, and no treatments. Despite this new tide of optimism, the obscured reality is that our older boys are loosing their lives to Duchenne.

The dark cloud became darkest about a year ago, when my son, then 17, had a routine visit to his orthopedist. After an examination of his back and an x-ray, the doctor informed us that his scoliosis had suddenly worsened compared to a few months ago. Because of the curve in his spine, his chest was being rotated and, as a result, was compressing the space available for the lungs and heart.

The doctor told us matter-of-factly that my son would need to have two rods inserted along his spine, routinely called spinal-rod surgery. After making the incision, the muscles are then stripped up off the spine to allow the surgeon access to the bony elements in the spine. The spine is then instrumented (screws are inserted), and the rods are used to reduce the amount of the curvature. He said that during the six hour-long surgery he would require a blood transfusion, since there would be much blood loss due to the incision along the back as well as in the bones. But he reminded us that surgery would give him a chance of living longer.

The doctor said we needed to act quickly due to my son's decreasing lung function, which is detrimental during surgery and recovery. I could swear the blood left my veins. I felt so desolate. After a visit to the pulmonologist, the go ahead was given. My son's lung capacity was at 40 percent. Although it is preferable to do this type of surgery when patients are younger and stronger, the doctor said if we acted swiftly, the surgery was still safe. He lectured not to wait too long, as lung capacity will get too low, and then the surgery will be more risky. He added that he couldn't guarantee anything. The doctor's words echoed loudly through my mind, my thoughts in a spiral. The idea of spinal-rod surgery induced a feeling of desperation and fear, the fear of my son possibly dying during this ordeal, and possibly dying if we didn't go through with it. And the recovery process, what about that? I didn't want to lose him. There was no guarantee he would make it. We were at a crossroad, an impossible predicament.

The bottom line was the horrific realization that we might lose our son sooner than we thought. We were damned if we did and damned if we didn't. How could I make such a decision?

For three months, my mind and thoughts were in turmoil, and the dark cloud followed me into my dreams. I was supposed to make a decision. How? I had so much advice designed to help me through my dilemma: "Pray," they said. "Through God you will know." "It is God's will," "I will support you." "It will be fine." "The right answer will come to you." "Reflect." "I know a good priest." "A swami." "A monk." "You must do it." "You must not do it." I searched through the chambers of my mind for answers and solutions. It was the most difficult time for me, the most difficult so far on this Duchenne journey. I was now facing head on the ugly reality of this cruel disease. The only answer that came was nothing. Did this mean no? Had the universe responded with a no?

After those months of what felt like an eclipse, I woke up one morning, and drew open the curtains and looked outside. I noticed the colors of nature, the sunshine. I looked up at the blue sky. I felt free. The dark cloud had gone.

I felt as if a weight had been lifted off me. I felt liberated, although nothing had really changed. I realized that the burden of the decision had deeply affected my happiness, my very nature. I acknowledged my internal conflict and let it go. I let all my thoughts go. I decided that I didn't want to fight and resist anymore with this disease. These were precious days and I still had my son. My perfect, sweet child of 17 was here with me, to touch, to hug, to love. Nothing was going to get in the way. We never did have the spinal-rod surgery. My son will be 18 in a few months. We are in the so-called "late stages" of Duchenne.

I was recently at a back-to -school night for my younger son, where parents and teachers get to meet and connect. I noticed during the five minute interval between classrooms, how the crowd of parents rushed along, headstrong, serious and focused and impersonal, not even stopping to say "hello."And then I wondered about the world of students, how in contrast they would amble along, chatting and laughing, carefree, drifting from classroom to classroom. I thought about my son with Duchenne, how he has missed much of this experience since he is home schooled, and how he may appear as an outsider. I reflected on his positive outlook, his radiance, and his mind so full of ideas and dreams. As I continue to navigate through this sea of uncertainty, I realize that I need to steer a less rigid course and to adopt a less serious way of thinking, and to enjoy the journey rather than worry about what comes next. After all, the future is something I have little control over. I stood somewhere in between the two worlds that evening of focused parents and carefree students. I stopped amidst the flow of the parents hurrying past me. I opened my arms wide, as if feeling for raindrops. Even though the dark cloud had gone, there were still going to be rainy days, there were still tough days ahead.

But I had a renewed lightness of being. At that moment, I realized that through my journey with Duchenne, I really had learned to dance in the rain.

Catherine Jayasuriya

Luke, 19 Years Old

Excerpt: "In Your Face Duchenne Muscular Dystorphy All Pain All Glory" ~Misty VanderWeele -Down To The Bone

Class of 2010

Luke had already been using his wheelchair for a few years full time as his muscles weakened and he lost strength, which is sadly the normal progression of Duchenne. He started favoring one side of his body more and his spine began to curve over, causing scoliosis. He was also becoming incontinent and having aches and pain he hadn't had before. Over time, if his back went untreated, Luke's left lung would most likely collapse. This meant one thing and one thing only. It was time to consider a surgical procedure called spinal fusion, where they insert and tie together two titanium rods down both sides of the spine.

Luke's father and I did a lot of research about the surgery and what would likely happen if we opted not to do it. We both felt that there really was no other option. The idea that these were our two options sickened me further and backed me into a corner, ripping my heart and mind right in two.

I had always felt that I would instinctively know when it was Luke's time to pass, but when I had to decide whether to go ahead with Luke's full spinal fusion surgery, my insecurities bombarded me and I wavered. So many questions loomed before me and I wondered if I had done everything possible for my boy. Would I lose my baby during surgery? Did we wait too long? What would life be like after the surgery? Would he still be able to feed himself? Any surgery is very risky for a DMD boy because of complications that can arise from the use of anesthesia.

These questions kept plaguing me and I often woke up sweaty and scared out of my mind. As I mentioned earlier, I had a premonition years before that Luke would not live past the age of 14 and, at the time of the surgery, he was not quite 15!

Another thing making me crazy about the surgery was the timing.. At the end of the summer, harvest in Alaska is in full swing and that meant that I would be facing Luke's surgery without Glen, my number one support person. I was absolutely terrified!

Once Luke went into surgery, the agony of waiting was excruciating and I was an emotional wreck. I sat waiting with my mom, my sister and my aunt. Luke's dad, Pat, and his new girlfriend, Bessie, sat in a windowed nook some distance away. Every so often, Pat would walk past me to the bathroom with a sick look on his face. The stress heightened when I looked up to find several of my family members all walk in at the same time, looking like they had lost their best friend. My heart dropped. "Did they know something I didn't?"

I found out soon enough that my family had just received news that a cousin had gone over a ravine in his car and was found two days later, alive, but in need of surgery. Ironically, he had been helicoptered to the same hospital and was waiting on Luke's operating room!

In all, Luke's surgery was 9 hours long. He spent a total of 8 days in the hospital and he only needed 8 weeks of bed rest at home before returning to school, instead of the standard 12 weeks normally required for recovery from such surgery. He healed very quickly. In recovery, I unexpectedly witnessed love in its truest form. The doctor had just removed the breathing tube from Luke's lungs and Luke was sort of freaking out. My ex-husband's girlfriend, Bessie, started rubbing Luke's hand with tears streaming down her face. My heart overflowed with amazement and joy at seeing another women, another mom, love my boy entirely! I was and still am delighted that Pat found a keeper.

During Luke's recovery at home, I was opening a can when the sharp metal circle came up and cut my finger. I actually heard it nick the bone! I was jumping around the kitchen, holding my finger and screaming, "I cut my finger, I cut my finger all the way down to the bone!" Luke said, "That is nothing, I'll show you down to the bone!" So true! Luke's scar starts at his neck and runs all the way down to his tail bone, where the rods were placed on both sides of his spine and screwed into his hip bones. When I first saw the stitches, I thought I was going to pass out! Another piece of my heart broken. How was that possible? I didn't think I had anything left in there to break!

With Luke resting peacefully, I went to take a shower in the "family" shower at the hospital, when I completely broke down, in shock from the horror of what my boy had just endured! What I had allowed to happen to him! But without the surgery, Luke would have been bedridden from pain and he would have had great difficulty breathing. If we had not straightened it, his spine would have slowly crushed his organs and lungs. It's a decision that no mother should ever have to make!

Misty VanderWeele
"In Your Face Duchenne Muscular Dystrophy All Pain All Glory"

Derek, 19 Years Old

Went to MDA clinic today. The doctor wrote in her charts, "Derek is in late stages of Duchenne Muscular Dystrophy." I told her that his pulmonologist doctor suggested it was time to discuss having a trach. I asked her if she knew anything about the non-invasive assisted breathing that Dr. Joshua O. Benditt at the University of Washington Department of Medicine performs. The MDA doctor said that would be a choice and went on to say that, when it comes to not being able to breath on their own, most young men, and their families caring for them, choose to do nothing and let nature take its course and let their bodies shut down naturally. The families let them die in comfort because it's too hard for families to take care of them 24/7. She said the state does help with some care provider hours, but not a lot. Their care disrupts the family too much, and the Duchenne patient gets too crippled and has no quality of life. The patients are just too hard too care for. I was shocked!!! My emotions almost took over. I felt like crying!!

You should have seen Derek's face! I was so proud of him! He chimed in and said, "Wouldn't their families rather have their family member with them than have them die? Wouldn't that disrupt the family?" I told Derek, "I am here to help you live. I am not here to help you die." I looked at the doctor and said that if Derek were 21, we would probably just go to the bar and have a couple of drinks after this clinic visit. The doctor said heartlessly, "Sometimes it's hard to talk about death." I said, "I know a lot of Duchenne families, and I have never known any that have chosen death over life."

Derek has been so scared of the trach idea and, in prior conversations, didn't want one. Up until today, he didn't understand how important it was. I looked at Derek while having this conversation and said, "Derek would want to get a trach if you couldn't breath?" Without hesitation, Derek looked at the doctor and said, "Yes,I would. I don't want to die." The MDA rep that was in the room was awesome. After the doctor left the room, I said, "I cant believe she said all those things in front of Derek." The MDA rep said, "The doctor just doesn't know how political you are about this disease. She doesn't realize how educated you are about Duchenne."

Summary: I don't agree with what this doctor said. I don't think most families just let their loved ones die. I do think this is what her beliefs are because she doesn't live it. I believe if a family just lets someone die, it's care provider neglect and child abuse. I will always choose life over death. I will support Derek through this journey. We will decide together on medical decisions. I will never give up doing everything I need to do to keep my son healthy and living. I couldn't imagine life without him!

Angela Turner

Timothy, 23 Years Old

A Hero

I had spread the sheet over the hospital bed, as I had helped the nurse remake a bed for my son, Timothy. As I was making his bed, I suddenly had a flash back of the 1980's, when I had worked hard for many years as a CNA in nursing homes and as a private duty nurse. I had gone to college for four years or more to be an elementary school teacher. I have even done some internship. Suddenly, I was doing nursing care for the elderly. I couldn't understand why I was doing this. This was not what I wanted to be or do in my life, but here I was, caring for the elderly. Bathing them. Feeding them. Taking them on walks. Taking them to recreation and physical therapy. How could I possibly be doing this type of work when my goal was to be a teacher?

It hit me as I was changing the sheets of Tim's bed. God had this plan for me. God was preparing me for Timothy. God was preparing me to be his caregiver, not just his friend, not just his mother. Tim just had spinal fusion surgery for his back to help him breath better. Although he was already in a wheel chair due to his illness, Duchenne Muscular Dystrophy, I was now, first, his caregiver, then, his mother. I was his friend who loved and cared enough to sacrifice all I had to help him survive this cruel world that knew very little or nothing of what Duchenne was about. I have been a single mother all his life. I have been caring for him since his diagnosis at the age of six years old. I suddenly became his voice. I suddenly became his advocate. I also had to be his father, his mother, his friend, his caregiver. I was his ONE voice.

Timothy is now in his early twenties. He has had a lot of challenges, but he has also had a lot of successes, too. From broken legs, surgeries, pneumonia several times and, now, living off a ventilator with a tracheotomy hanging in his throat so that he can breathe better, he has graduated from high school with a high GPA and has attended one of Florida's best universities, the University of Florida. Timothy is a fighter. He has chosen to live when life was throwing death at him.

A few years ago, while at a treatment center, a therapist told me that most likely my son will live only for the next six months. At first I agreed that she was right, but then it hit me. It really hit me. I locked myself up in the women's bathroom, weeping. I had fallen down, begging God to please spare him and to take me instead. I was mentally lost to the idea that my son's illness could possibly take him into a deep, dark world from which he never could return.. I was suddenly very angry. I was suddenly very confused and lost. How could I live my life without him? He was my best friend, not just my son. He was the light, the joy, the comedian of my world. I was totally heart-broken. I was frightened for him. I prayed it would not happen until many years from now.

I can recall that in 1995, his teachers in first grade were noticing some unusual things about Timothy. I had noticed it years earlier but thought he was just being a boy–lazy with poor coordination. He had a hard time getting up from the floor. He couldn't roller skate. He couldn't climb stairs. He couldn't play on the skate board. He had large calves. I just thought he was being lazy. But the teachers and the school nurse knew more and suggested he see a doctor.

Timothy's pediatrician knew right away what was going on and showed me information about Duchenne in a book. I think at the moment I was shocked, in denial. No way did he have this. We began the testing process after seeing his neurologist. From the muscle biopsy to the nerve testing, it was all too much for me, and for him. It was too overwhelming.

Then one day the call came in, the call that would tell me there is no cure for this disease and that most likely my son could die by the time he was twenty years old. My son was diagnosed with Duchenne Muscular Dystrophy. I remember feeling totally shocked. I remember my mind also going a thousand words per minute. I remember weeping. How can this be? Why Timothy? And how do I tell his father that his only son may die within the next 10 years?

We have faced so many challenges since his diagnosis. Not just mentally and physically, but emotionally and spiritually. It became a struggle for us. We slowly watched family "running" from us instead of supporting us, him. This included his father. It was like our biggest fear was not just his diagnosis, but family not wanting to deal with this. It was new in our family. We had no history of Duchenne in either side of the family. It was like no one wanted to be educated or know. It was like they were more afraid of the disease then he was.

Over the years I have learned how our physicians, our nurses, our educators, our family, our friends, our community seem to be so ignorant about this disease. It has shocked me that they know very little of muscular dystrophy and how to treat it. I realized more and more that we need not only more education for the medical field, but that our community really needs more awareness.

I have struggled over the years knowing that my only child may pass away from this illness. You will always grieve for your child. You know there will be a loss even if, right now, he sits in front of you. You try to put those thoughts away and enjoy him at that moment. But it's like every time he is in the hospital for cardio or respiratory issues, you fear this will be the end. But so far, I have seen my son fight for his life. He does not want to give up and die. He enjoys his life, even it means sitting in a power chair and playing on the computer. I know eventually he may go. But I don't want him to go. So I fight this disease with him.

Timothy, you are my hero!

Dee Bird

Ben, 26 Years Old

What If

What if you had a beautiful baby?
What if the baby was diag nosed with a disability?
What if the disability was terminal?
What if all your hopes and   dreams were gone?

What if you grieved a little each day?
What if you looked at life differently?
What if you appreciated all the little things?
What if you found new hopes and dreams?

What if the baby grew up?
What if you were nervous about letting go?
What if the other kids were mean?

What if he fell a lot?
What if he got hurt?
What if he got his first wheelchair?

What if we can't handle this?
What if you adjusted to each level of worse?

What if he graduated from high school?
What if he could go to college?
What if you found a college with 24-hour care?
What if he went to college?

What if the college experience forever changed his life and yours?
What if he found independence, friends, and a social group?
What if he went bowling at 2AM?
What if he dated?

What if things you never imagined were possible?
What if he wanted this independence when he came back home?
What if you found many others who wanted this same independence?

What if we worked hard to make this happen?

What if it were called the Independence House?
What if he can live on his own?
What if dreams came true?

What if this is what he was born to do?
What if the doctors were wrong about life expectancies?
What if we never let go, never dreamed, and never asked, "What If?"

Postscript:

Ben is now 25 and has Duchenne Muscular Dystrophy. He attended and graduated from Edinboro University of Pennyslvania, where he discovered independence we never thought possible. This journey has changed our lives.

We started The Independence Foundation 5 years ago and now have two houses where physically disabled individuals live self-directed lives. Ben has been living on his own now for three years! It is amazing what is possible once it enters your reality!

Christine Muller

Andy, 28 Years Old

I just keep losing stuff

"I hate this damn disease! I just keep losing stuff!"

Andy is sobbing, just sobbing, and he hates it. He hates it, not because he doesn't want to cry. No, he needs that. He knows it's time. It doesn't come easy, and it doesn't come often. But it's time, and he needs to let it out. He hates it because he can't wipe away the tears, can't blow his own nose.

Andy is 28, an age that affords him the dubious distinction of being what's known as a DMD Pioneer, someone who is beating the odds, living beyond the usual life expectancy of mid-teens to early twenties. It also means he's had a lot thrown at him, more than most people will ever have to deal with. Somehow, despite all this, he wakes up every morning with a smile on his face. Every day starts the same way--always cheerful, always in a good mood. As his father and primary caregiver, I thank the Lord for this, while wondering how in the world he does it.

"I hate this damn disease! I just keep losing stuff!" he sobs. And he does. I understand. At nine, he lost the ability to walk. At eleven, he could no longer bathroom himself. At seventeen, he could no longer write. This was about the same time that he lost the ability to feed himself. At twenty, he got a tracheostomy. He could no longer breath on his own, and he's been on a ventilator ever since. When he was twenty-four, Andy had a gastronomy tube installed in his stomach. He could no longer swallow properly. Eating had lost its joy, becoming nothing more than a chore. Andy had lost the ability to eat.

And now, today, another loss. He could no longer operate the trackball on his computer. One of the few constants over the years has been his computer.

Around the time he stopped walking, Andy went to a couple of Orlando Magic basketball games. We couldn't afford to take him often, but the Muscular Dystrophy Association occasionally came through for us with free tickets. For Andy, this was heaven! The fact that he was in a wheelchair suddenly didn't mean another activity he couldn't enjoy. Quite the opposite-- it meant he got special treatment. He got into the arena early and, at times, got to go down and meet one of the players. He got an autograph or two, something his able-bodied walking friends didn't even have. He was hooked immediately and has remained over the years a basketball fan extraordinaire.

Realizing that he could never actually play basketball, Andy did the next best thing. He watched all the games he could, followed the teams, got to know the players, checked their stats, and became the ultimate fantasy league fanatic. After a year or two of joining fantasy leagues, he started his own, a hobby that he could participate in right on his computer. Eventually, this spilled over into football, where he became even more of a fan, running leagues, joining pools, and placing the occasional bet.

So here he was, frustrated once again by the fact that his muscular dystrophy was once again robbing him, taking something away. "I hate this damn disease! I just keep losing stuff!"

I think that's probably the hardest part about living with Duchenne. It doesn't discriminate. No matter what you do, or how you attempt to treat it or deal with it, it simply marches on. Just about the time you've learned to cope with the last loss it's handed you, it smacks you upside the head with another.

Families of DMD boys know this. They all learn this lesson. When Andy was first diagnosed, his mother and I vowed that we wouldn't let Duchenne run our life. We would do everything in our power to make sure Andy's life would be as full and as normal as it could possibly be. I think every family makes this same promise, whether consciously or not. It's a form of denial, I suppose, or perhaps simply naiveté. And as admirable as it may seem, it's simply not going to happen. You may be able to keep up the facade for a while, doing the things that every family does. Family outings, vacations, camping trips, or whatever. But at some point, Duchenne begins to rob you, and there's no stopping it. It marches on.

Please understand, I'm not trying to paint a picture here of doom and gloom. Far from it. Our boys and our families can still have a good life. But it will never be what most people would consider normal, not even close.

Like most young people, the week that Andy graduated from high school was one of the most exciting of his life. He moved into his own apartment. A place that was his, a place that gave him what every kid that age wants. Independence, or at least a semblance of it. Since he could no longer do simple things like dress or feed himself, independence was a relative term. He needed a full time live-in caregiver. But that wasn't the point. Here was a place he could call his own. He got to call the shots, not mom and dad. For Andy, it was seventh heaven. Two years later, of course, Duchenne marched on and robbed him once again. It was time for a tracheostomy.

Boys with Duchenne Muscular Dystrophy eventually succumb to either respiratory or cardiac failure. When Andy was twenty, he was always tired. Sleep studies determined that this was a respiratory issue. His lungs simply weren't supplying enough oxygen into his blood stream. In an effort by his own body to make up for this, his heart worked overtime at night, when it should have been resting.

While the tracheostomy resolved Andy's respiratory issue, it caused another problem. Now his caregiver had to be trained for trach care. Andy lives in Green Bay. The state of Wisconsin, and in particular Brown County, has always been a leader in the area of long-term care for the disabled and elderly. But even here, keeping up with the kind of long-term care required for an advanced case of Duchenne's is nearly impossible. Trying to find and retain the kind of dedication it takes on a 24-hour basis simply doesn't happen. The family has to step up.

Let's take a look at a typical day. Typical for Andy and his caregiver, that is, far from what most would consider normal. As you read this, try for a moment to think about it from his perspective. You can talk, you can move your thumbs, and you can operate a computer with speech recognition. Other than that, you have no movement whatsoever. What would you like your caregiver to do for you first? Caring for Andrew is a 24x7 job, more than most people can imagine. It's tough. You are absolutely on his clock, always, and believe me when I say it's a rather abnormal clock. I try to get up around nine to have some time to myself and get a few things done. Andy usually sleeps until ten or eleven, when I let his dog (Buddy, a beagle) into his room to wake him up by planting big, sloppy dog kisses all over his face. We then spend about three hours in his room before he gets out of bed. I start off his day by hooking up the first of his three tube feedings, which he calls "pork chop in a can." For the first hour or so, he often reads or gets on his computer for a while. If he reads, it's often on a laptop, which is much better than when he reads a real book – no pages for me to turn every 90 seconds!

After that first hour or so, I bathe and shave him, toilet him, dress him, and switch his ventilator over to daytime mode. During the day, his vent assists his breathing. At night, it does it for him completely, which means he can't talk. I've gotten quite good at reading lips in the dark. We also do a cough treatment during this time--20 or 30 reps on a machine that forces air into his lungs and quickly pulls it out to simulate a cough. This loosens things up in his lungs and trach.

Finally, around two in the afternoon I get him into a sling lift, bathroom him, and put him into his wheelchair. We then head to the bathroom to brush his teeth and wash his hair. When that's done, we usually head outside for 5 to 10 minutes with the dog. In the summer months I sometimes hook the dog leash to his wheelchair so he can walk the dog up and down the alley behind his apartment building.

Between three and four, I start another tube feeding, and I try to eat something myself, do dishes, laundry, pay his bills, etc. Usually he'll either watch a movie or have me put him on his computer, where he'll spend an hour or two talking trash with his fantasy football and basketball buddies, do a few emails and download music. It takes a good 5 to 10 minutes to get him situated properly. He used to be able to use a trackball mouse, but now does everything using a microphone and speech recognition software. Sometimes I try to sneak in a nap, anywhere from 30 minutes to an hour, depending on how much sleep I got the night before.

Around seven, we bathroom him and start getting him back in bed. The TV goes on with one of his many movies, or perhaps a game. Football is now his game of choice, followed by basketball or baseball. Or he may hop online for a while on his computer. I use this time to grab some dinner. At eight, I hook up his final feeding, then join him in his room for a night of whatever he decides we're going to watch on TV. Around nine, we do another cough treatment, and, around ten, we start the switch over to his ventilator's nighttime mode. Adjusting to this takes quite a while. Much of this time is spent using a suction machine to get the secretions out of his throat and airway. That's constant, all day and night, but especially from eight until about one or two in the morning. A little after midnight, I bathroom him again, and, some time around 12:30, I turn off his light and leave his room. I seldom go to bed myself until at least two or three, because he'll call me back into his room (he can still press a call button with his thumb) about every 10 to 15 minutes until then. Some of that is suctioning, and some of it is just, "I'm cold," "my nose itches," or, "please move my legs for me." Anyway, two in the morning is a good night. Bad nights can go until five, six or seven. Sleep deprivation is a constant and brutal enemy.

Probably the hardest part of this job is being trapped here in his small apartment. I can't go any farther than the range of his baby monitor, even placing it in the window when I take his dog out or go down the hall to do the laundry. Andy knows it's tough and teases me about it. When I first moved here, he put up a sign for me that said, "Welcome to Shawshank." He has a great sense of humor, which helps. We do have some fun, and despite the tough schedule I've described, I thank the Lord for the relationship He's giving me with my son. Andy must tell me twenty times a day, "I love you Dad." How many men get that from their 28-year-old son?

We also thank God for those 28 years. The prognosis for Duchenne boys is a life expectancy of late teens to early twenties, so we call these his "gravy years." All of Andrew's friends that he went to MD camp with over the years died by the time they were 17. Anyway, I think I've given you the gist. What it boils down to is that beyond everything I've described here, there are tons of things I can't describe. Scratch an itch (100 times a day), suction my trach (50-75 times a day), move my arms, raise my legs, rub my shoulders, get a blanket or heat a corn bag ("I'm cold"), clean my glasses, dial the phone for me, start a movie, turn up the stereo, get me some ice water, and on, and on, and on. Your time isn't your own--ever. It's a 24x7 job, more than most people can imagine. The one constant is that Duchenne keeps marching on. Andy, his caregiver and the whole family just keep losing stuff.

Despite all of this, despite everything Duchenne can throw at you and everything it takes away, caring for Andy is an enormous blessing. I love my son dearly, and short of a cure, I wouldn't have it any other way. It's a hard life, but it's beautiful.

Jay Keller

Todd, 22 Years Old

A Poem from Cathy Gould Harrison
Founder and President of Defying Muscular Dystrophy

A Mom's Journey

Time to have a baby, unknowingly guided down my road,
A baby boy was born, reaping the seed that I had sowed.
A special bond enveloping my heart, euphoria did I meet,
My life was filled with happiness, the world was at my feet.

Loving my sweet, precious baby, and oh, wanting to have more,
But alas, the crack of doom began, for pregnancy became a chore.
Second time wasn't so easy, what could possibly be wrong?
Third time passed by fruitlessly, this was taking just too long!

Memories creeping in from past, uncle, brother... thoughts of long ago.
This can't be real, it's just a doubt, but soon I'd really know.
The waiting, praying, crying, worrying tore me inside out,
When that spirit-breaking day arrived, I knew not what life was about.

Grieving as though I was dying, cycling through and through,
Moving through the motions, never really knowing what to do.
Grabbing the reins inside my hands, declaring I would not be beat,
Life would not control my path, my ego wouldn't accept defeat!

Throwing myself into adoption, silently denying the pain,
Waiting and waiting and praying that a baby would we gain.
God ever so gently hinting to me, that this was not my way,
But I refused to listen to him, so unwilling to accept delay.

Meeting and loving that baby who would forever change my life,
Never, ever knowing how this experience would cause me such strife.
Holding that innocent babe in my arms, to have her from me tore,
died yet again... a painful death, I could not take any more.

My spirit was completely broken, something I had to allow,
For then something changed deep within, and did I graciously bow.
I said to him, "My life is yours. Just where will you have me go?"
And he answered to me, "To go forth.... and within you, I will show."

Anxiousness permeating throughout my empty soul,
I felt I had nothing left to give, my heart had become a hole.
Not wanting to live with any of this, waiting for it all to end,
Whispering feelings spoke to me, "You will be able to bend."

Living through depression, slowly gaining strength from God above,
I knew it was not from me; it must be Him who willed me love.
For in his eternal wisdom, he guided me to my end,
Not knowing that until I was stripped, would my desires begin to ascend.

It wasn't until I accepted life and held no more hope or gain,
That my life began to build again and ease the horrendous pain.
Glimpsing--finally--a rainbow, could this really be true?
I was truly pregnant with child, never having had a clue.

Soaring the heights of blissful happiness spiritually in my soul,
Earthly emotions remained on guard, oh, life had taken its toll.
My daughter was born, I was still so numb, was this all a mistake?
Once again, my intuition was right, PLEASE, oh, Lord, don't take!

Yet once again, He answered me, and in time I came to know.
That He was the one who carried me and still whispered He would show.
My children's lives were in his hands, nothing for me to do.
What I thought I emotionally barred myself from—Love came shining
    through.

Realizing, finally--once and for all, to turn to Him in strife,
Because now I know that he as a plan, for EACH of us in life.
It happens simultaneously, both choice and circumstance,
It seems our lives our dually planned for us, yet also left to chance.

Wherever our lives lead us, however long they last,
This life is but a school for us, and earthly time goes fast.
Oh, Lord, whatever happens, I can only remain close to you,
For only through death comes birth again.
    It was something I learned of YOU!

Cathy Gould-Harrison

(Todd is afflicted with Becker's, a slighter form similar to Duchenne.)

SECTION IV
Rest In Peace

By far this is the hardest section I have written. Writing through tears and a personal view that has hurt me more times than I'd like to remember is never easy. If you have made it this far, you have laughed, you have most likely cried, you've taken the emotional roller coaster ride Duchenne parents and their families live every day. You have witnessed the amount of courage it takes to face Duchenne of a son. But mostly you have learned each of these boys grace each family in very raw and authentic ways. Each of them carry something special with them, a certain spark of personality and silent strength that speaks louder than words.

I've heard many times from the older guys living with Duchenne say their bodies feel heavy and stiff with shallow breathing very aware of every heart beat. -Actually they are slowly suffocating, no muscles left to breath until the body can no longer live.Now before you go on, make sure you have tissues near by for the next set of stories, for you will never be the same.

Nick 1992-2009

"Kiss me on the forehead, give me a hug, and I'll do the same to you."

The date was August 11, 1992

The day my life took a dramatic turn, little did I know my life would never be the same. Life as I knew it had changed, and there was no going back. Oh, how I wanted a girl. I had two boys so, yes, I wanted a girl. Yet, when I saw my beautiful baby, with his blonde hair, tiny fingers and tiny toes, I fell in love. Nicholas Michael Davis, that is what my husband at the time and I named him. When he was just two days old, we were told to "prepare" ourselves because something was terribly wrong with this beautiful baby. It could be his heart or he could be bleeding internally. The pediatrician was not sure, but one thing was for sure. Our baby was very sick, and though we did not know this at the time, our beautiful baby was not expected to live!

Nicholas was born with four holes in his heart and needed a coarc repair. One week old equaled surgery. Two weeks old equaled more surgery. Nick ended up having a pacemaker (which is a story of its own). At five weeks old he came home. By the time he was five years old, he would be like any other five year old, his cardiologist told me. Little did she know that my beautiful son had Duchenne Muscular Dystrophy. Little did any one know that Nick had this devastating, life-taking disease. When Nick was five months old, he went to Maine Medical for a heart catherization. After receiving succinyl, Choline, Nick went into cardiac arrest. My husband and I were told that that the only people who would react to this anesthesia were people who were allergic to it or had a muscle disease. Since my husband and I had two healthy older boys, the doctors did not think that it was a muscle disease. However, when the blood tests came back, we learned Nicholas had Duchenne Muscular Dystrophy. How could so many things be wrong with one little baby? And why?

When Nick was little, I tried most days not to think about the deadly muscle disease my son had and prayed every day for a cure. Hope and prayer are what I relied on. He was little and we thought time was in our favor. Nick started to walk at three years old. I remember when we first moved to the home were I live now. We were excited to finally have a house and a house where each of the children would have his own room. My husband at the time, John and Nick and I were outside, where the play yard was going to be. I looked up and our Nick had taken off way up a hill out back of the yard. Although I ran to get him, I was smiling inside because he had walked so far. I still look back to that day with a smile on my face. Nick always loved girls. I tried to keep Nick's life fairly normal, although this was hard. So many issues to deal with, but I'm proud to say that Nick became the kind of person people loved to be around. He loved people and they loved him back. He had such a wonderful attitude and he knew he was so loved. He brought smiles to people's faces, with his sense of humor his honesty and his up-beat attitude. Nick had wonderful teachers and teacher aids. Nick also had many wonderful nurse's whom he loved very much. Joanne, Judy and Prue were three of the nurses that were working with him in his teenage years. They were more than nurses. They knew what was important to Nick and always made time for those things. Holidays were VERY important to Nick. Nick pretty much knew of every holiday there is, and he wanted to celebrate as many as he could. I'm not exactly sure why, but Halloween was his favorite!

Nick started to use a wheelchair part time when he was 11 and 12 years old. By the time he was 13, he started using it more and around the age of 14 years old, he was using the wheelchair all the time. At first, Nick did not want to use a wheelchair, but soon he preferred it. When Nick was 14 years old, he granted a wish by the Make A Wish Foundation. He picked beautiful Australia. Nick loved to travel and we traveled quite a lot. When Nick was 15 years old, he had a terrible accident. It was right after Christmas, and my sister was visiting us. Nick had some gift cards/money. We took Nick to a book store (Nick loved books). Nick was holding onto his books and he was not buckled into his wheelchair. As I took him down off the curb, Nick feel out onto the pavement! Talk about feeling guilty; I still feel guilty today for not having him buckled. Nick was in so much pain. He broke his femur. He was taken to the hospital in that city. When they saw how bad the break was, they gave him so many pain killers that later that night he got very sick. The next morning, I called for an ambulance. Nick was taken to our local hospital. The pediatrician said he was very sick and needed to be taken to Maine Medical Center in Portland. The doctor there said Nick had aspirated into his lungs. He had an acute lung injury, and there was a good chance he would not live. I was in total shock. How could he go from a broken leg to fighting for his life? During his time in the hospital, Nick's lung collapsed, and I just remember saying to the doctor, "He is not going to die." It was a waiting game. While Nick was fighting for his life, back home my first grandchild had been born, Cade Ethen Davis. Nicholas was finally able to come home with a full leg cast, and with a lot of help ,things eventually went back to "normal."

Nick was around 16 when things started to go down hill quickly . He lost interest in eating and soon weight became an issue. Nick was getting weaker and weaker. By the time Nick's 17th birthday came around, I had seen quite a change in his health, and not for the better. Nick needed a feeding tube put in, plus he needed a pacemaker change. We had Nick's birthday party and then had the feeding tube put in. The whole feeding tube thing was hard. Nick was on 24 hour feeding. He finally had gained a couple of pounds and weighed around fifty pounds. The plan for school was to have Nick get the feeding tube put in, pacemaker changed. He would be tutored at home until spring, due to his becoming weaker and due to the possibility of being exposed to germs that came in the winter time. Halloween came around and Nick had a party. He went to a few houses trick or treating. As long as he went, that's all he cared about. Well, the time came for Nick to get his pacemaker changed, and he was to come home either later that day or the next day. "The surgery went well," the surgeon told us. Nick was on a tiny amount of oxygen, so he needed to spend the night in the special care unit. Nick used a bi-pap machine at night, so he could not go to the children's unit. "I want to go home," Nick kept hollering. My son, Chris, and I took turns spending time with Nick, because he did not like being alone. Nick watched television, read books ,etc. So we all figured he'd be home for Thanksgiving.

The next thing I know, I was staying at The Ronald McDonald house with my son, Chris, and my mom, when the doctor called early in the morning and said they might need to put in a breathing tube. I rushed up to the hospital. Friends from our church came, Nick's dad and his wife came, and my other son, Paul, came. I called my sister, and she and her husband flew to Maine. Soon, so many relatives and friends were at the hospital. We were told Nick did have to have the breathing tube put in. The plan was not to keep him on it very long because, the longer we waited, the harder it would be to get him off the breathing tube. I knew in my heart that this was it. I was in shock, Nick's dad and I had already agreed that we did not want Nick to live on machines. The tube was taken out, and one by one friends and family went in to see Nick, who was unconscious but seemed to be resting peacefully. Soon it was me; my sister April; my brother-in-law, Paul; my niece ,Angel; and her boyfriend, Steve, sitting with Nick, telling "Nick" stories. Angel, Steve, and Paul went to the cafeteria, and my sister went and asked the nurse how Nick was doing. She said he would pass within the hour. April quickly called the Ronald McDonald house and told everyone to come to the hospital right away. With April and me sitting alone with my beautiful son, whom I love with all my heart, Nick soon took his last breath. April saw angels all throughout the room. She saw Nick and my sister, Cathy (who died as a young child). Nick looked at her and smiled, and then he and Cathy walked forward together holding hands, while angels filled the room. Me? I crawled in bed with Nick. My wish was to hold him after he passed since I hadn't been able to hold him for years. Still in shock, I told the nurse to take out all tubes and wires. I wanted to hold my baby. I rocked Nick for four hours, and I could have held him forever.

It has almost been a year. Some days it feels like yesterday, and other times it seems like a lot longer. The hell I have gone through this past year is something I wouldn't wish on my worst enemy. I live in the moment, get lots of counseling, and faithfully go to a support group for parents who have lost a child. I wish I could say I'm all right, but I can't say that because I'm not. I suffer from a broken heart. This disease that robs children of their right to feel free to run, jump, to play sports, to not feel the fear of dying young, this disease that causes parents the torture of watching their child get weaker and weaker needs a cure. When I see Winnie the Pooh items, Power Rangers, Teenage Mutant Ninja Turtles, Scooby Doo, and books (there were many books Nick loved to read), I miss my little boy. When holidays come, all these things make me miss my little boy even more (if that's possible). I will see Nick again, and that keeps me going.

Priscilla Davis (Nick's mom)

"If ever there is tomorrow when we're not together ..there is something you must always remember. You are braver than you believe, stronger than you seem, and smarter than you think,.but the most important thing is, even if we're apart... I'll always be with you."

Winnie the Pooh

Peter

Excerpt: Intensive Care ~Mary-Lou Weisman

"*Help!*" I yell out loud. "I'm cracking up," I say more softly. The moment I hear my words, I know them to be true. Here, in the middle of the night, when the rest of the house is sleeping, is when I can hear myself think. I sit up, bring my knees under my chin, wrap my arms around my legs and stare into the fireplace.

Something's got to give. I just can't do it all. It would be easier if I were willing to have live-in help, but I'm not. I've tried six different housekeepers so far, and they've either quit or been fired or run away. There have been two runaways so far. That's how much they like me, too. It just doesn't work out. I don't let it work out.

I let them clean and shop for groceries and do the wash, but I won't let them take care of Peter, not really. I'm always listening in and intervening when I hear tempers flare because, after having responded cheerfully through almost five minutes of regrets and painstaking adjustments to Pete's sleeping position ("Fix my ear on the pillow; it's folded under." "Tuck my right hand more under the pillow."), they find he *does* have to pee, after all, and they'll have to start all over again.

"Please don't be angry, please, I'm sorry, please," Pete begs them. The worst thing for Pete is if you're angry with him because it's then that he fears you may desert him, leaving him alone to experience his own helplessness.

I suppose I could try once more. I could put an ad in the paper under "Help Wanted" or maybe just under "*Help!*" I would write the job description very carefully so as to weed out in advance anyone who wasn't right for the job.

Live-in person to help care for ten-year-old boy, wheelchair bound with muscular dystrophy. Must be loving and cheerful. Must piss child and turn him during the night. Must take the trouble to prop a pillow under his right elbow so that he can hold his penis himself, even though that takes more time. Must cut his food and swoop it through the air like a roller coaster into his mouth, sometimes swerving off at the last minute to fly it into her own mouth instead, to give him something funny to complain about. Must open his bureau drawers each morning and hold up his shirts and trousers, one by one, until he chooses what he wants to wear. (He is getting to that age when he cares about how he looks, especially at school.) Must brush his teeth and not mind if he bites down on a finger. He does that only to show himself, and you, how strong the muscles in his jaws still are, even though the rest of him is wasting. Must, after school, when he tires of entertaining himself by drawing or listening to records, be willing to tell him stories, sign old camp songs, dance around the living room like klutzy Marakova to Chopin polonaises, or shave his face with aerosol cream and Daddy's empty razor. And if all fails, as sometimes happens, and you sense that a shadow has fallen across his soul, and you know that even you cannot make the sun shine, must hold him in your arms and tell him that you love him, and lift his arms and fold them around your neck so that he can tell you that he loves you too. Best salary for the right person.

Of course I've rigged the ad so there can't be any takers, so there isn't any "right" person but me. But there isn't. With all the arrogance of love, I believe that. Nobody else is good enough. Even I'm not good enough.

It's not that I'm determined to be a martyr. It's not that I don't struggle to free myself from my fate at the same time as I embrace it, that I don't sometimes wish Peter dead while I pump life into him, that I don't dream of leaving him while I dig myself in deeper. Even Peter walks in his dreams.

Postscript:

Peter Weisman: 1964 –1980

Yesterday was Peter's birthday. Had he lived past the age of 15 ½, he would now be 46 years-old. My husband Larry and I can hardly believe that he has been dead for 30 years, twice as long as he was alive.

But we don't like to think about a 46 year-old Peter. What would he look like? Would he still be so funny? Would he be married? What would his wife be like? What would he have chosen for his life's work? Would he have children? Would he be content with his life? We recoil from all futuristic thoughts about Peter as unnatural, verging on grotesque. Our Peter was and is forever young–an infant, a baby, a boy, a teenager. Period.

In retrospect, we do not think of his life as cruelly shortened by Duchenne Muscular Dystrophy, although, of course, it was. We think of his life as complete and full and happy. For 15 ½ years we devoted ourselves to making his life worth living in spite of the unrelentingly downward spiral of Duchenne, and we believe we succeeded.

I mourned Pete most profoundly the day he was diagnosed at the age of 2 ½. That was the worst time of all. But after a period of weeks, during which I knew nothing but unremitting sorrow, I began to find my way back into life. I tried to imagine that, if we were living in the Stone Age or maybe medieval times, a life as short as Pete's was predicted to be, would be normal. Surprisingly, during Peter's life span, I seem to have accomplished that sleight of mind. Although we contributed as much money as we could afford to research that might save Peter's life, we never counted on a medical rescue. Instead, like all the parents of children afflicted with Duchenne Muscular Dystrophy, we had to count on ourselves to make our son's life worth living, day by day. We had to measure success in quality, not quantity. We had no choice.

But focusing on quality didn't spare us the lash of sorrow. There is no comfort for parents who must preside over their child's slow dying. Life with Peter was a lot more painful than life without him. Every day that he was alive, I grieved for him, even as I did everything I could to be cheerful and make his life normal and happy. My marriage nearly failed. Our older son, Adam, suffered from having too little attention and too much responsibility. Larry and I lived in a fog of exhaustion, anxiety, depression and mutual recrimination with occasional time-outs for love and understanding. I rarely got a night's sleep. Sometimes I thought I was going to lose my mind. Often I wished Pete dead. Does that confession shock you? Try this one. When Peter died, my first feeling was relief. I was dry-eyed at his funeral while our friends wept. They assumed I was in shock. I wasn't. I was at peace and so, at last, I hoped, was Peter.

But time does not heal all wounds, and peace and relief turned out not to be the end of weeping. I was wild with grief and hollowed out by loss. I was lonely for his love, his self. I would visit Pete's room and bury my face in his pillow or his clothing to breathe in his essence. These ghostly sessions always brought me to tears as I held Peter's empty clothing in my arms. Ultimately, time took away all sensory clues to the living Pete. It was time to strip the bed and give his clothes to Goodwill. Pete was gone in body, but not soul. A new, permanent stage of mourning had begun, accompanied by healing.

When I meet people for the first time, the conversation invariably gets around to, "Do you have children?" After I answer "Yes," I steel myself for the tough question– "How many?" I always answer "Two," and hope the questions will stop there, but too often they don't and, ultimately, I am obliged to face the awkward situation I have created and to explain that our younger son is dead. I know what's coming next–a flood of sympathy and discomfort. "Oh, how terrible," and "I can't imagine anything worse," or "Oh I'm so sorry I asked," as if their question had reminded me anew that my child was dead. They may be feeling sorry for me, but, in fact, I am feeling sorry for them. I take no pleasure in embarrassing total strangers who have every reason to believe that they are engaging in a safe, social ritual, by tripping them up this way, but I refuse to deny Peter's life and his abiding importance in my life. I continue to love him and be proud of him in death as I loved him and took pride in him during his life. I have two children.

It is thirty years later and I think of Peter every day. Sometimes my thoughts are casual–Pete would have liked . . . or Pete would have said . . . . But sometimes thoughts, unbidden, cut me to the quick and bring me to tears– "Pete, where are you? I miss you so much." Peter's favorite stuffed animal and sleeping companion, a large, soft gray hippo whom Pete named "Soft Gray," is now our sleeping companion. Every morning when I make the bed, I give "Soft Gray" a hug, conjure up Pete's sweet freckled face, and hold his hippo long enough for tears to fill my eyes, before I place him against my pillow. I enjoy these tears. I make them happen. They link me to Pete. Mourning Pete is a way of having Pete.

I talk to Peter every night before I go to sleep, as if he can hear me. I tell him my troubles, as if he could help me. I ask for his blessing as if that could soothe my soul. He is a vital part of my life. He makes me happy. Believe this.

Mary-Lou Weisman
Author of *Intensive Care*

Visit www.marylouweisman.com for more information

Ashley

I sit here now and I wonder,
Wonder if things will improve,
Wonder if a cure will be found,
Before more people have to lose.
The pain these people go through,
I cannot comprehend.
I wish that there was something I could do,
Something more then lend a hand.
People need to realize, and people need to learn too.
I saw it through my brothers eyes, and this I share with you.
A boy trapped inside a shell, a boy that had dreams,
A boy who never thought of himself, a boy that was never mean.
He was an angel sent down to us,
Sent so we could be aware,
Aware that through all this pain, we still had love to share.
Sent to help us realize, and sent to give us hope, too,
That someday in the future, their suffering will be through.

~Maggy Simpson

In memory of Ashley Adam Kirkham who had Duchenne Muscular Dystrophy.

One Story

A Word from Patricia Furlong
Founder of Parent Project Muscular Dystrophy.

I don't have an active story about Duchenne. My story is now painted on the walls of my heart and photographed on my mind. My sons were diagnosed over 20 years ago. It came as a surprise, as we thought we had no reason to worry when having our children and in our innocence thought we had some guarantee of health. We had no experience with rare genetic disease. In fact, we believed catastrophic events happened to the other guy. We were blissfully unaware.

Duchenne has taken my sons from this current life, but not from our thoughts or our memories. The walls of our home echo their laughter–our laughter. The walls of our home have wheelchair marks. We look at the scrapes and dents as gifts and reminders of our boys. The walls of our home reflect our family and we, as a family, feel blessed; blessed to have had our sons and yes, blessed in many ways by Duchenne.

Chris was our thinker. He was thoughtful, considerate, and always a planner. He loved school and was a serious student, number one in his class in most things and worked hard to stay at the top. One other student, Tom, sometimes scored higher. Chris would start the conversation, "I did ok" (meaning nearly perfect) "but Tom ...", indicating Tom edged ahead, sometimes by one single point. Chris loved math and biology. He had to fully understand how things worked, often figuring out geometry problems in his head before putting them on paper.

His biology teacher assigned all the students an ethics paper. Chris' paper was to be focused on "suicide for the terminally ill." I was incensed. I tried speaking to this teacher calmly, then less calmly, then screaming. No teenager should be assigned such a paper, especially a teenager with a terminal illness. To this day, if I say her name out loud, it feels like I am spitting. In my fantasy world she is fired, retired, and sorry. Chris, the brightest one of all, simply ended his paper with his opinion—a single sentence: "You have no right to destroy what you didn't create." And while, in so many ways, our boys with Duchenne are immature, they are all wise.

Patrick was our lighter side. Openly, we referred to him as a smartass and an inciter. He could enter a room, quickly identify everyone's hot buttons, and, one by one, push each person to their limit. His visit would often end with someone yelling "PAAAAAAATTTTTRRRRIIIIIICCCCCKKKK!!" and silence. I would hear the click of the wheelchair, a soft chuckle, and tires rapidly moving on to the next event.

Patrick loved school. Each day was treated as a new social event. He made plans on top of plans. Each year his school held an auction. Jewelry, trips, sports paraphernalia were on the auction block. Patrick asked for a blank check, "just in case," he would say. Of course, he would not spend much. Of course, he was mindful that the blank check had to be accompanied by an account with sufficient funds. Of course, he knew. But he was planning. One of the items up for grabs was to be coach of the basketball team. This would be his, no matter the price. He was bidding against ten people and the amount got fairly high--into the low thousands. With a smile, he shouted "I'll take it! I have a blank check from my mom!" Thankfully the bidding ended and Patrick was to be the coach. "And mom," he said with a smile, "you don't have to buy cookies for the next few weeks."

Life with Chris and Patrick was often difficult, the care overwhelming, and the therapeutic nihilism appalling. There was no internet, no Google search options, no NIH or Pub Med available, and no Duchenne community to guide our path. But, we celebrated each step forward and loved our time together. We did not have enough time together, but what we did have is treasured. We had to say goodbye way too soon.

Each day, I speak with my boys. It is my inner monologue. Some might consider it praying. I ask for their help, for their guidance. I ask them for instruction, for ideas about how to increase awareness, how to make the world know about Duchenne. I ask them for help. Often in the quiet I hear something, a soft whisper. Sometimes it's an image or sometimes a dream. And there are times, in the midst of my often animated conversations, that I know they must be smiling.

I frequently complain to Chris and Patrick about the lack of awareness about Duchenne. I talk about the stories I hear from the families, how they try to explain Duchenne (how do you explain a catastrophe?) to people they meet. I talk about the anger and letdown when friends confuse Duchenne with MS. It is just so aggravating and all of us lose patience and sometimes friends in the process.

My conversations can take off in one direction or another and I'm certain, when this happens, the heavens roll with laughter. Recently, in my discourse, I decided Congress and perhaps all of the governments in the world should write new laws. These laws would forbid any individual from using their name to describe a disease or disorder. I would demand they use proper terms to describe the condition in order to avoid confusion. Drs. Duchenne and Becker would have to understand that we were removing their names for a specific purpose. Instead, we would say our sons had Muscle Cancer.

Now, some might argue about the differences in cellular pathways from cancer to 'Muscle Cancer,' but I'm guessing the public would have more of a visceral response if we said our sons have Muscle Cancer. The word cancer strikes fear in the heart, any heart. Questions are serious: where, what treatment, what now, what will happen? There would be no confusion, no risk of silly comments suggesting that "he does not look sick." Rather, the public would sit up and take notice. They would learn that muscle can get "sick" and would make the natural association to functional loss. It might just be an "ah-ha moment" and wake up the world. It may well cause enough consternation to increase resources and incentivize researchers. It would require breaking barriers across related conditions and result in thinking in new ways. It would help us buy time: time that we dream about, time to make additional memories, time to dream. If only I made the rules...

"There is an alchemy in sorrow. It can be transmuted into wisdom, which, if it does not bring joy, can yet bring happiness." - Pearl S. Buck

Pat Furlong

You have just met 40 sons who have Duchenne Muscular Dystrophy, some of which are no longer with us. Duch-enne is a progressive muscle disorder that causes loss of function and independence. Duchenne affects 1 in 3,500 boys. To date, there is no cure. We are working to change that. To learn more about the Duchenne Movement or to support our cause, please visit:

MistyVanderWeele.com

Or One Of These Duchenne Organiztions

Jett Foundation – jettfoundation.org

Kingston, MA
Phone- 781-585-5566
Christine McSherry – President
info@jettfoundation.org

MDA – www.mdausa.org

National Headquarters -Tucson, AZ
Phone: 1-800-572-1717
You can also find local contacts on their website using the zip code locator tool.

PPMD - parentprojectmd.org

Hackensack, NJ
Phone – (201)-944-9985
Toll Free – 1-800-714-5437
Pat Furlong – Founding President and CEO

Kimberly Galberaith – Executive vice President
Email: Kimberly@parentprojectmd.org
Ryan Fischer – Director of Community Outreach and Advocacy
Email: ryan@parentprojectmd.org
Will Nolan – Director of Communications and Administration
Email: will@parentprjectmd.org

Coalition Duchenne - coalitionduchenne.org

NewPort Beech, CA
Phone – 714-801-4616
Email: Cahterine@coalitionduchenne.org

Cure Duchenne - cureduchenne.org

Corona Del Mar, CA
Phone – 949-872-2568
Email – debra@cureduchenne.org
Debra Miller – President

Who is Misty VanderWeele

I was born and raised in Alaska. Actually I still live here, surrounded by wide open vegetable fields at the same time protected by the mighty Alaska mountains with my husband, our daughter and my son. Even as a little girl I knew Alaska was where I wanted to raise my own children. The great Alaska outdoors full of camping, 4x4's, hunting, fishing and snowmobiling was the lifestyle I wanted. So when my son at 4 years old was diagnosed with Duchenne, a muscle disease that would rob him of his muscle function, be wheelchair bond by 10 and most likely not live to graduate high school, broke my heart into a million pieces of shattered dreams. No parent should *ever* have to go through that.

So life dealt me lemons, the next obvious step for me was to be the best mom I could be by getting to work making not just lemonade, but margaritas. Providing a quality of life for my son was the most important. I also intuitively knew through my struggles with my sons disease I could help and inspire other people, especially those touched by Duchenne to live the best lives they can.

My first taste of providing such inspiration, was a year after my son's diagnosis when a journalist who wrote an award winning article about my son and I titled *"On A Wing And A Prayer"* with the caption; *A mother and son fight a deadly disease with faith, hope and a positive outlook.* The journalist had this to say about us *"meeting them had a profound impact on me because their courage and positive outlook must take incredible strength"*. Reading her words left me with a feeling of awe in how all the pain my son, family and I was going through wasn't for nothing. Even today, some 15 years later, I still feel the same way. Inspiring others is my life purpose.

I am a Partners in Policy Making graduate, a Duchenne advocate and have several years network and internet marketing, website design, web 2.0 experience under my belt. I also have 15 years of disability workshops, speaking, fundraising and endless sleepless nights on the roller coaster of pain Duchenne causes. Witnessing your child's body deteriorate before your eyes is not easy thing to endure, especially having to face the probable outcome of an early death.

Oh, did I mention I am an author too? My first book *"In Your Face Duchenne Muscular Dystrophy All Pain All Glory"* I wrote for my son as a high school graduation gift. It is a living memoir of his first 18 years of life fighting Duchenne. Wanted to write his life out while I still had him with me. And yes, here in 2010 he will be 19, a huge mile stone in itself that I wouldn't trade for anything!

Writing *"In Your Face"* I realized there has been over 50 years of Duchenne research with steroids still being the "standard of care" and no effective life saving treatments to speak of. That somewhere along the way Duchenne, the most common childhood life taking muscular dystrophy, with 20,000 new diagnoses every year, was still practically unheard of . Meaning boys are still dieing from this horrible disease and nobody knows. Which is absolutely unacceptable! I also wrote about the Duchenne Movement and how I wanted to contribute to assist in the ultimate movement that will create a CURE once and for all. I even learned how to build my own website/blog, www.MistyVanderWeele.com.

After review and research of other diseases that have been cured and world problems that have been solved, I have found a common thread in how answers and success is achieved. There is always a "team" if you will or meeting of the minds, a group of people who come together, put their differences aside for the greater good of all. And that is why I wanted to create this very book *Saving Our Sons One Story At A Time*, full of Duchenne parent stories to show the world something has to be done about ending Duchenne; not just for my son, but for ALL our sons.

Misty VanderWeele
MV International
MistyVanderWeele.com
PO Box 4124 Palmer Alaska 99645
mistyvanderweele@gmail.com
Facebook: facebook.com/mistyvanderweele
Twitter: mistyv & duchennemom

Honored Duchenne Sons of Past

Michael Bryan Rivera, September 21, 1980 – February 20, 2007

Ronnie-Ronald Michael Shatto November 19,1985-June 6, 2010 Son of Catherine & Danny Shatto Springfield, Ohio

David Keith Flinspach, Date of Birth: 10-23-1980 Date of Death: 2-26-1999

Alexander McDonald, August 12, 1992 to November 29, 2009

Tyson Nicoll - 26.12.1990 - 20.08.2010

William Rossiter, 8th October 1998 to 1st June 2009. rest in peace little guy.

Joseph James Sands, April 28, 1959 - September 12, 1974

Robert Thomas Stanitis 6/26/84-3/12/06

Jeffrey Joseph Polinski 5/10/82-4/26/05

Allen E Fairchild, was 28 when he lost his duchenne battle...July 28 1967-Nov 12 1995

Sony Tomlinson, 12 years old 6/10/1997 - 4/9/2010

Misty Gives Back

A portion of the proceeds of *Saving Our Sons One Story at a Time* is going to the story contributors who have chosen to participate in the affiliate writer program. Such affiliates selling books will be able to cover expenses insurance won't cover, give to the Duchenne charity of their choice or use towards something special for their son/sons. Hereby the commission they earn will be spent at the affiliate writers digression.

Contributors

Seven of the stories in this book were taken from previsouly published sources, such as books, blogs, essasys and facebook. Please note the ad pages in the back of the book for further information.

The remainder of the stories were contributed by Duchenne parents, sibling and a grandparrents. Many of which are writers, duchenne advocay blog owners and not-for-profit founders.

Heather Meermann: I am a wife and the mother of two boys with a baby girl on the way (due Jan. 2011). My youngest son Grant has Duchenne Muscular Dystrophy and we are on a mission to save his life. I have a journalism degree, taught elementary school for 5 years, and have a graduate degree in psychology with licenses as both a Nationally Certified School Psychologist (NCSP) and a Licensed Specialist in School Psychology (LSSP). I currently work part-time with our charity, Save Our Boy Foundation, to help raise funds for Duchenne research. Heather Meermann Save Our Boy Foundation Fighting to End Duchenne Muscular Dystrophy www.SaveOurBoy.org

Julie Hicks Hathaway: I am the proud wife of Bobby Hathaway and mother to three beautiful children, Amber 12, Brandon 8 and Ethan 3. Originally from Eastern North Carolina, my husband and I were transferred to Greenville, South Carolina in 1995. I am currently a part time reading interventionist at Mauldin Elementary School, where Brandon is a student, and work with at-risk kindergarteners in the area of reading. During my years in education, I've been a principal, assistant principal, teacher evaluator, adjunct professor, mentor, and classroom teacher, all of which I have enjoyed tremendously. I have and education degree from East Carolina University and a Master's in Administration and Supervision from Furman University. I enjoy scrapbooking, boating, and spending time with family and friends. I am a member of Standing Springs Baptist Church where I teach Sunday School and volunteer when needed. My family and I are also a Safe Family to families in our community who are in need. I am passionate about helping to find a cure for Duchenne Muscular Dystrophy and am always looking for opportunities to raise awareness and money for this disease. Please feel free to contact me at lynnlee@charter.net<mailto:lynnlee@charter.net> or give me a call at 864-325-8338. Julie Hathaway Reading Interventionist Mauldin Elementary School 355-3794 jhathawa@greenville.k12.sc.us" We teach children, not subjects."

Heather Clower: I am the wife of Marty Clower, and mother of Cooper and Adam Clower. I graduated from University of Southern MS in 2001 with a degree in Psychology. In 2004, I opened Dreamworks Gymnastics Academy in Ocean Springs, MS. God blessed us with Cooper Lee Clower in 2006 and Adam Christopher Clower in 2008.

Deni Eubanks: My son Brayden Eubanks is 7 years old. He was diagnosed with Duchenne Muscular Dystrophy on April 1st 2010. To look at this sweet boy you would think that nothing is wrong with him, but on the inside he is being destroyed. I have decided to write our story so that other familes going through the same thing can see that they are not alone. Although this is a devastating thing that has happened we know that there will one day be a cure. Hopefully sooner than later. We as a family with familes need each other where you have been going through this for years or just days there are always questions and concerns. We need awareness, and A CURE NOW!!

Perlita Hains: is a wife & mother. I am a marketing professional working in the physical therapy field and truly adore my work. I have three spectacular sons,Luke 10, Lance 8, and Levi 4. My husband Gordy & I have been married for 16 years and have enjoyed almost every minute of it!!! I decided to contribute a story about our early journey to help me remember how far I've come as a mother and how far we've come as a family. The road is tough, tougher than most but we are finding our way through the maze.The maze of questions, medicines, clinical trials. It's our world now but not all consuming. We are living a phenomenal life and making happy memories for all our boys. Levi's muscles may never be as strong as his big brothers but his 5 pack is STRONG, very, very STRONG!!!

Leigh Alisen Pernosk:has been a California girl all my life. I am the wife to an amazing man, and Mommy to 2 precious boys. I am living my dream as a stay-at-home Mommy and feel so blessed with all the gifts God has given me. I want to do anything I can to help get awareness out there regarding Duchenne Muscular Dystrophy to save my son's life & the lives of anyone suffering with this disease. I'm honored and happy to be a part of helping create awareness about Duchenne Muscular Dystrophy, we hope to see a cure for this disease in the near future.

Leeandra Archdeacon: Is a Woman who walked the road of infertility, struggled with the fears of adoption and now fight ing for her sons life. http://nicksjourney-leeandra.blogspot.com/

Sal Acrchdeacon: Is a proud husband and father of two children. Growing up in the Monterey Bay in a large Itlalian family has taught him the importance of life.

Brenda Burk: is 39 years old and lives in Pennsylvania with her husband Justin and three children. Brittany, Hunter and Caitlyn. Brenda has a small child care business in her home.

Jane Williams: I'm a loving mother of two beautiful boys,who love camping,cooking,art,swimming and spending time with friends. I have a fabulous husband and a wonderful life, Duchenne has made us appreciateour family and friends more and experience each day Life is precious make the most of it. Oh and by the way my 10 yo has duchennes (almost forgot).........

Sharon Gonzalez: Where to start, it's been a rough past couple of years between my son getting sick constantly and my husband going to Iraq for a year..and now this diagnosis. My 8 year old son was diagnosed with Duchenne's Muscular Dystrophy in the summer of 2009. On July 10, he had blood work drawn to see which type it is exactly- DMD or BMD. The results came back as positive for Duchenne's Muscular Dystrophy. My husband and I are just heartbroken and full of tears. It's still difficult to hold back tears. He is our only child, his name is Nathaniel. He is such a sweet and loving boy, he hugs me quite often and kisses me on the cheek every single day even if I don't ask for a kiss, even if I'm asleep, he'll come and give me a kiss good morning or good night on my cheek. He is a cuddle child and I love every minute of it! He says I love you all the time and blows kisses and gives me tons of hugs before getting on his school bus every morning, hard to leave and go to work, knowing I'll miss him coming home from school. My husband will retire from the military in 2 years. But meanwhile, we are spending every minute with our child, just enjoying him and living in the moment. These journal entrees I submitted for Saving Our Sons was created in hope of finding a cure for Duchenne's Muscular Dystrophy and to spread the word about the symptoms of this disease to other parents. There is no current cure for the disease, so God will be the one to cure my son. I am a mother, a provider and a military spouse. My husband is currently deployed in San Diego, California and I reside in Fort Worth, Texas. We have been married for 10 years.

Laura LaPat: is a pastor's wife and mother of 6 children, one of whom has DMD. Laura is a stay-at-home/homeschooling mom, trying to educate herself about Duchenne. She feels that this book will help others by seeing that they are not alone in the fight with this disease. She has a blog called Boy Blessings (www.babyloveblessings.blogspot.com).

Rhiannon Ramkissoon: I was born in Orange County, CA and now live with my husband Christopher and our son Carter Blaze in Riverside, CA. Life can be crazy for us at times, but we strive to live each day to the fullest. I keep a blog to document Carter's journey; www.adventuresofcarterblaze.blogspot.com. I can also be reached by email at: cure4carterblaze@gmail.com.

Amanda Rudd: I am 29 years old and live in Ohio. I have a wonderful 8 year old little boy, named Cade who has DMD. I am a parent advocate for the Duchenne Community and this has been my life for three years. This is very important to me because I hope to one day find a cure for this disease and we can look at it as a thing of the past. Also, I hope to raise awareness so people understand what it is like to be in our shoes and why it is so important for a cure for these boys. My story is sincere and straight from the heart, I want people to enjoy and have hope that with love and faith all things are possible.

Michelle L. Jones: Is a graduate of The Ohio State University and is a 20 year dedicated employee of the Ohio Division of Wildlife. She enjoys giving and helping others. Traveling with her daughter Malia, her son Kelvin and her husband Henry, to Henry's native home of Belize, Central America, and other destinations, is what she enjoys most in life, as it makes her smile when she spends time with her children; watching them learn about animals/cultures/places and especially enjoying life. She has vowed to never give up, until a cure/treatment is found for Duchenne Muscular Dystrophy. You can reach Michelle directly at Emelita1@aol.com.

Kim Maddux: I live in Northern CA with my husband and 3 kids. My oldest child, Alex has Duchenne Muscular Dystrophy. I love to read, scrapbook and spend time with my family and friends. I was inspired to share my story to bring awareness to this disease that has affected so many wonderful families. My hope and prayer is that a CURE is found soon for all of our children.You may contact me at kim@manda.net

Suzanne M. Desmond: is a mother of a son with Duchenne Muscular Dystrophy and Autism Spectrum Disorder. I would like to say thank you to Misty Vanderweele for giving me the opportunity to share my sons story. I watch my son struggle with not only with his body, but his mind and would do anything to stop that struggle, but at the same time Francis always has a reason to smile at least once a day. I am not sure that a cure will be found in his lifetime, but will not give up hope or give up trying to find a cure not only for Francis but for others like him as well. Not only do I raise awareness for DMD but just as important for ASD. Autism should not be ignored in a patient with DMD, but as part of the patient and directed to someone/organization for therapy to deal with the ASD and help to make their lives more manageable.

Naomi Clark-Dessender: Is a daughter, a sister, a wife and most importantly, a mother. This book is extremely important to me because when my youngest son, Joshua, was diagnosed with this disease, and we had never heard of the words Duchenne Muscular Dystrophy before. My life want is to have these three words as well known as cancer is, with treatments just as common.

Lisa Edmonds: I don't work outside the home, I'm Cam's carer, have tried to get a job, but being too honest, I tell them about Cam and I don't stand a chance! So have decided to give up trying, and concentrate on throwing myself into fundraising. I have done lots of fundraising in the past, and I am also a card maker, and I sell them for cams cause. I am at present, taking a year out from both, as soon we will be moving to a bungalow for ease for Cam, so busy getting sorted for that. It's a scarey thought, as we're moving to another borough, and also nearer to cam's secondary school which he will be starting in September! The years have flown since I had Cam, he's our only child, and I will keep raising those funds in the hope of one day finding a cure, if not in time for Cam, then hopefully one day for others. This book means alot, because it's getting the message out there, and making more people aware of duchenne muscular dystrophy, something which, before Cam was diagnosed I had never heard of, and when strangers ask, I find most have never heard of it before.

Lisa Jones: Is the mother of Bradley Jones, a 13 years old with Duchenne Muscular Dystrophy. She has a daughter, Stephanie Jones, who is 17 years old. Her husband of 20 years is Tom Jones. Lisa and her family reside in Southern Illinois.

Stephanie Jones: is the sister of Bradley Jones. She is a Senior in High School and plans to go into Nursing as a career. Her inspiration for going into nursing is her experiences with her brother, the nursing background in her family and a desire to help people. In her free time, Stephanie enjoys writing short stories, poems and songs.

Debra Miller: I was born in a suburb of Los Angeles and lived there until I moved to the beach cities of Orange County during high school. I graduated from UCLA with a BA in Communications Studies. Most of my career was in technology publishing, starting out as an advertising sales representative for *Computer World* and moving on to a position with Cahners Publishing in Boston working on *Mini-Micro Systems* magazine. I joined Ziff Davis Publishing as the Regional Manager for *PC Magazine* and was fortunate to be there during the record breaking growth of that publication. With the growth of home technology, I moved to a Scholastic publication, *Home Office Computing*. I took time off when my son, Hawken, was born and then resumed my career working as an independent stock trader. When Hawken was diagnoses with Duchenne, my husband and I founded CureDuchenne in 2003. Since then, I have worked full time (plus), first as a volunteer for 6 years and then as an employee. I wear four distinct hats at CureDuchenne, scientific director, business development director, marketing director and administrative director, since CureDuchenne is focused maximizing the dollars we send to research. CureDuchenne has contributed to six research projects that have progressed to phase 2 or phase 3 trials. Our mission is our name...to Cure Duchenne, the most common muscle disease in children. www.CureDuchennne.org

Donna Mckenzie: My son Ryan is 13 yrs old and has DMD. I wanted to be part of this book because when my son was diagnosed we weren't given any information. We felt totally alone, and I don't want any other parent to feel that way. Knowledge is power and the more we can share about our children and what they go through the more likely we are to get people involved in helping to find a cure. I can't do big things but I can do this, in honor of my son.

Alan Thomas: is a civil engineer and works for Luke Air Force Base in Phoenix, Arizona. Jolie Thomas is a special education teacher but stays home and takes care of Callam. We have a daughter, Savannah, who is a freshman at Arizona State University. Of course, there is Jay, Callam's assistance dog and Blue. He's the boss.

Catherine Jayasuriya: draws her inspiration from her three wonderful children. Her eldest son suffers from Duchenne Muscular Dystrophy, and the challenges this has brought has been a catalyst for her to live in the present moment and to live with gratitude. Catherine is Malaysian/English. Her father is part Kadazan and part Sri Lankan, and her mother is English. She was raised in Kota Kinabalu, in the Malaysian state of Sabah on the island of Borneo. She has lived in Malaysia, England, Australia, Canada and currently in the USA, but still calls Sabah home. Catherine has undergraduate degrees in Asian History and Photojournalism, and a Masters in Psychotherapy. She's a mother, singer-song writer, author, photojournalist, psychotherapist, traveler, animal lover, environmentalist and yoga enthusiast. CathJayasuriya@yahoo.com

Christine Muller: is the president of The Independence Foundation. The Muller Family started The Independence Foundation in March 2005 to help their son gain independence. After graduating from college, there were few options for living independently. A staying with parents, a nursing home or group home were the only choices available. The Muller family set out to establish housing where individuals with disabilities coudl live independent, self-directed lives. The Independence Foundation currently owns two homes in East Aurora, NY where 7 young adults live. Ben has been happily living on his own now for almost four years! We never dreamed that this would be possible! Contact us at cmuller@theindependencefoundation.org

Dee Bird: Born in the concrete jungle of New York, Dee has spent most of her life traveling after attending a Christian Boarding school. In 1988, becoming a single parent, she choose to keep her son and gave birth to Timothy in April of 1989. They have traveled before settling in Maryland. Dee received her AA degree by attending Montgomery College. In1993 they moved to Florida where they now reside. Tim was later diagnosed withDuchenne Muscular dystrophy. It this through this diagnosis that Dee began to advocate…not only for Tim but the many children who needed more attention then just the MDA. In 2000 she tried to start an organization on Publicity/Awareness of Muscular dystrophy. Due to funding, the organization closed down. Since then she has been a full time caregiver for her son and advocating on his behalf. She believes that if DMD has much more awareness and much sooner that a cure might had been found sooner with the correct amount of funding. This book is a resource and tool to help bring more awareness and tell the amazing story of our boys of their courage and bravery as they battle this terrible illness, and as they fight for their lives. This book is dedicated to all the brave boys who have fought the battle and lost to the disease but left us with more knowledge and understanding for that cure!

Cathy Gould-Harrison: Is the owner and CEO of JIR Enterprises, Inc., Jump Into Reading, a Supplemental Educational Service Provider. My company contracts with California school districts to provide after school tutoring. I hold a Bachelor of Arts Degree, California Teaching Credential, and a Master of Arts Degree in Reading Instruction. My son, Todd is a 3rd generation Muscular Dystrophy family member. For me personally, I need to experience real progress in the fight to cure and end all forms of Muscular Dystrophy. To be witness of 3 generations in my family is beyond heart breaking. On of our family members lost his fight. Collectively, we need to make some noise and this book is an awesome opportunity to do exactly that. The time is NOW!

Jay Keller: I'm Andrew's father. Andy is what's sometimes called a DMD Pioneer, one of the boys who's beating the odds by living beyond Duchenne's life expectancy.

I gave up my career 3 years ago to become Andy's fulltime caregiver. While doing so has been difficult, it's also been a blessing beyond words. Andy's mother Kathleen Lewis and his sister Bobbi Estupinan share in this joy by taking over for me on weekends. We welcome comments or questions, especially from the parents of younger DMD boys, and can be contacted via email at Jay@AndysHouse.net.

Priscilla Davis: For 17 years I have been truly blessed to be called Nick's mom...I got married very young and have three boy's...Christopher is 26 years old, Paul is 24 years old, and Nicholas would be 18 years old...My oldest son is married to my wonderful daughter in law Ary and they have my two adorable grandchildren Cade 2 years old and Eban one years old...Life can be very hard but I know some day I will be with my son Nick again and that keeps me going....Nick always had a smile on his face and was a blessing to all that knew him...I hope you enjoy and learn from my short story about my life with Nick, for there isn't a day that goes by that I don't miss him.

Pat Furlong: is the Founding President and CEO of Parent Project Muscular Dystrophy (PPMD), the largest nonprofit organization in the United States solely focused on Duchenne muscular dystrophy (Duchenne). Its mission is to improve the treatment, quality of life, and long-term outlook for all individuals affected by Duchenne through research, advocacy, education, and compassion. When doctors diagnosed her two sons with Duchenne in 1984, Pat immersed herself in Duchenne, working to understand the pathology of the disorder, the extent of research invest-ment, and the mechanisms for optimal care. In 1994, Pat, together with other parents of young men with Duchenne, founded PPMD to change the course of Duchenne and, ultimately, to find a cure. Today, Pat continues to lead the organiza-tion and is considered one of the foremost authorities on Duchenne in the world. In 2010, Pat was named WebMD's Health Hero and was featured in *The New Yorker* as a "World Changer." She is the recipient of Research!America's 2008 Gordon and Llura Gund Leadership Award.

Maggy Simpson: I am 24 years old. My brother Ashley Adam Kirkham had Duchenne Muscular Dystrophy and was sadly taken away from us on 18th February 2010 aged 27 Years. Ashley started to write a book about the condition and how it affected him - I would like to finish the book in memory of him. Tilted 'Through thick and thin, A life with Duchenne.' As I cannot say it from his point of view it will be a siblings point of view which is also where the poems come in. This condition has a great impact on everyone, as it did with all our family. The pain and hurt we still feel so raw even after nearly a year. My peoms are a way to express the way the condition affects those who have it and their families, but also try to get the reader understanding that although these boys/men have this condition they are still normal people with normal everyday feelings.

Permissions

Mary-Lou Weisman: www.marylouweisman.com It was my second son, Peter who inspired my first book, Intensive Care: A Family Love Story, originally published by Random House in 1982 and now available on line in paperback. Peter died of Duchenne in 1980. I was determined to keep his spirit alive and to offer to others a totally honest, unsentimental account of how our family overcame the shock, grief, anger and marital stress that the Duchenne diagnosis brings. I am happy to have an excerpt from Intensive Care and a retrospective post script included in Saving our Sons, One Story at a Time. Sharing our experiences makes us and our children stronger.

Since then I have had other books published, most recently a biography, Al Jaffee's Mad Life (2010; HarperCollins); a best-seller, My Middle-Aged Baby Book (1995 Workman Publishing Co.) and its sequel, My Baby Boomer Baby Book (2006 Workman Publishing Co.) as well as Traveling While Married (2003 Algonquin Books). My essays, feature articles, interviews, and film and book reviews have appeared in many magazines, among them The Atlantic Monthly, The New Republic, Newsweek and Vogue. I have written syndicated columns for the New York Times, "One Woman's Voice" and "Hers." I have also contributed commentary to Public Radio International.

My husband Larry and I remain active in the Duchenne community by participating in what we believe is the most promising organization devoted to ending Duchenne --Parent Project Muscular Dystrophy (PPMD)

Angela Turner: I am married and mother of three beautiful children. two daughters and my son, Derek who is 21. Derek graduated in 2009. My son was diagnosed with Duchenne Muscular Dystrophy at the age of 4. Duchenne Muscular Dystrophy doesnt run in our family and I am not a carrier. Living with DMD has been an emoitional and heart wrenching roller coaster. My career is working with disabled and high risk students, for the school District 9th-12th grade. I have worked there for 15 years. As of last

September I have resigned my position. I needed to be home to care for my son. I want to make sure he is happy and has the best care possible. I am happy to share one of my many horrific experiences."MDA Doctors Visit", to help other DMD families who are fighting this dreadful disease, I want other families to be prepared, who have not reached this far in the Journey of DMD. l want them to know there are other options. I also want to help educate others, so people will understand what DMD is and what DMD families deal with on a daily basis. I want the whole world to know how much I love my son. I want the whole world to know how important it is to save all of our children, suffering from this devastating disease. My son is running out of time! I can't imagine life without him. I pray a cure is found Today.

Penny Wolfson: "Moonrise," First published in The Atlantic Monthly, December 2001. Reprinted by permission of the author. Penny Wolfson won a National Magazine Award in 2001 for the essay "Mooonrise" and is the author of the book of the same title, published by St. Martin's in 2003. Her work has appeared in The New York Times, the Atlantic Monthly, Good Housekeeping and a number of literary journals and magazines and has been anthologized in Best American Essays, 2001, Love You to Pieces, and STories of Illness and Healing: Women Write Their Bodies. She has taught nonfiction writing at Sarah Lawrence College and Columbia University and is a member of Columbia's "Future of Disability Studies" group. Ansel is now 26 and works in New York at the Confucius Institute at Pace University. He and Penny have often spoken publicly about his disability and about Duchenne; both will be members of a panel at Barnard's Feminism and Disability conference in February.

Rita Zondlo Felling: "Josiah and Cody" First published http://behindmysmile-raf.blogspot.com/2010_01_01_archive.html January 29, 2010

Rita is an advocate, volunteer, aspiring writer and single mother of three sons, residing in Fridley, Minnesota. Rita first began living with Duchenne Muscular Dystrophy over 40 years ago with the diagnosis of her three brothers. Today, she continues this heart wrenching journey as she watches Duchenne, once again attack, this time claiming her two youngest sons, Cody and Josiah. Rita as a single parent gives us a glimpse, through her writing, of the strength, tears, joy and heartache Duchenne has brought into her world. She currently is in the process of finishing her memoir "Tears of Strength: a single mother's life long journey with Duchenne".

Charlotte E. Thompson, M.D. is a board-certified pediatrician who in 2003-2003 was named as one of the Top Pediatricians in the United States for Pediatric Neuromuscular Disorders by the Consumer Research Council. She has directed six neuromuscular programs and is an Assistant Clinical Professor of Pediatrics at University of California Medical School in San Diego. She is the author of *Raising a Handicapped Child* and *Raising a Child with a Neuromuscular Disorder* and also a mother and grandmother. FindingGoodMedicalCare.com

Duchenne Parent Blogs

Boy Blessings
Behind my Smile
A Mom's Journey
Jill Anne Castle
My Son, My Rain
Navigating Through Life
Adventures of Carter Blaze
The Accessible World
Cure Dales Duchenne

"Extraordinary Story of Love, Determination and Bravery"
~Debra Miller CureDuchenne Founder

In Your Face Duchenne Muscular Dystrophy...

All Pain...All GLORY

"A Beacon of Light for Others With the Same challenges"
~Patricia Boeckman

"This book will serve as a handbook to many and will have a HUGE impact
on the world of Duchennne~ JBT

Quality paperback $17.95

E-Book Available June 2011

Order Online
MistyVanderWeele.com

Intensive Care

"One has to be a superb writer to lift the story about the wheelchair that Peter Weisman was confined in from his seventh year and waltz around with it so brilliantly. But that is what Weisman, who vowed that 'Peter's life must grow steadily and bravely upward,' has done. There are times when the power of Weisman's prose squeezes the heart like a sponge, but perhaps the best moments leave you laughing."

—Phyllis Theroux, *Washington Post*

"Weisman manages to bring a desperate humor to *Intensive Care* without undermining its awful seriousness."

—Anatole Broyard, *New York Times*

"This is an exhilarating book about life, love and joy as well as about sadness and death. Mary-Lou Weisman has been twice brave – first as a mother, then as a writer. It is wonderfully written; probably you will read it without getting up from your chair."

—Robert and Suzanne Massie

CPSIA information can be obtained at www.ICGtesting.com
Printed in the USA
LVOW071759191011

251139LV00002B/117/P